# Copy and Reference Puzzlers Book 3

128 FUN Puzzles

Jason Turner

# Copy and Reference Puzzlers Book 3

128 FUN Puzzles

Jason Turner

ISBN 9798817268737

# Also By Jason Turner

C++ Best Practices

Object Lifetime Puzzlers Book 1

Copy and Reference Puzzlers Book 1

Opcode Puzzlers Book 1

Object Lifetime Puzzlers Book 2

Object Lifetime Puzzlers Book 3

Copy and Reference Puzzlers Book 2

# Copies and References

This puzzle book focuses on value copies and references. You'll have to trace what values change when a new value is assigned.

The goal of this puzzle book is to use as few words as possible. Instead you will learn how to do the puzzles simply by looking at examples.

Important note:

Anything starting with // is a "comment" and has no impact on the code!

## A Note On Puzzle Layout

Some puzzles split across pages. Sometimes this is annoying. I've decided to leave it how it is because it adds a sense of realism to what it's actually like to read unnecessarily complex C++ code.

## How C++ Relates

Each of these examples are real C++ code. If you are a C++ user, you can learn more about object lifetime with these puzzles.

Each solution is a topic that has something to do with C++. If you cannot figure out what the solution means, then duckduckgo for it and learn something new :).

If you aren't a C++ user then don't worry about any of this, just have fun!

## About Jason Turner

Jason is a developer, speaker, and trainer who specializes in C++. His goal is to make C++ as approachable, fun, and accessible as possible. This book is part of that effort. Jason can be contacted via emptycrate.com. Be sure to check out his YouTube channel, "C++ Weekly."

# Values

### Value Example 1

```
void run()
{
  print("5");
}

// Answer: 5
```

### Value Example 2

```
void run()
{
  print("{}", 5);
}

// Answer: 5
```

### Value Example 3

```
int value()
{
  return 5;
}

void run()
{
  print("{}", value());
}

// Answer: 5
```

**Value Example 4**

```
void run()
{
  int value = 5;
  print("{}", value);
}

// Answer: 5
```

**Value Example 5**

```
void run()
{
  print("{}{}", 4, 2);
}

// Answer: 42
```

# char Puzzles

**Puzzle 1**

```
void run() {
  char char_1{'q'};
  char_1 = 'm';
  char char_3{'j'};
  char_1 = 'v';
  char char_5{'a'};
  char_5 = 'q';
  char char_7{'c'};
  char_7 = 'w';
  char char_9{'s'};
  print("{}{}",
        char_7, char_9);
}

// Answer (2):

// __ __
```

**Puzzle 2**

```
void run() {
  char char_1{'g'};
  char char_2{'c'};
  char_2 = 'w';
  char char_4{'v'};
  char_1 = 'v';
  char char_6{'r'};
  char_2 = 'e';
  char char_8{'o'};
  print("{}{}",
        char_8, char_6);
}

// Answer (2):

// __ __
```

**Puzzle 3**

```
void run() {
  char char_1{'c'};
  char_1 = 'x';
  char char_3{'f'};
  char_3 = 'd';
  char char_5{'q'};
  char_1 = 'a';
  char char_7{'v'};
  char_7 = 'e';
  char char_9{'e'};
  char_3 = 'x';
  char char_11{'e'};
  print("{}{}{}",
        char_9, char_3, char_1);
}

// Answer (3):

// __ __ __
```

**Puzzle 4**

```
void run() {
  char char_1{'n'};
  char_1 = 'h';
  char char_3{'j'};
  char_1 = 'l';
  char char_5{'f'};
  char_3 = 'i';
  char char_7{'y'};
  char_7 = 'j';
  char char_9{'e'};
  char_1 = 'n';
  char char_11{'y'};
  print("{}{}",
        char_3, char_1);
}

// Answer (2):

// __ __
```

**Puzzle 5**

```
void run() {
  char char_1{'m'};
  char_1 = 'c';
  char char_3{'l'};
  char_3 = 's';
  char char_5{'q'};
  char_5 = 'u';
  char char_7{'s'};
  char_5 = 'a';
  char char_9{'t'};
  char_7 = 'k';
  char char_11{'r'};
  char_1 = 'e';
  char char_13{'w'};
  print("{}{}{}{}",
        char_3, char_1, char_9, char_13);
}

// Answer (4):

// __ __ __ __
```

**Puzzle 6**

```
void run() {
  char char_1{'t'};
  char_1 = 'q';
  char char_3{'l'};
  char_1 = 'g';
  char char_5{'q'};
  char_1 = 'l';
  char char_7{'m'};
  char_3 = 'v';
  char char_9{'k'};
  char_1 = 'c';
  char char_11{'l'};
  char_9 = 'e';
  char char_13{'n'};
  print("{}{}{}",
        char_11, char_1, char_7);
}
```

```
// Answer (3):

// __ __ __
```

**Puzzle 7**

```
void run() {
  char char_1{'u'};
  char_1 = 'g';
  char char_3{'j'};
  char_3 = 't';
  char char_5{'u'};
  char_3 = 'n';
  char char_7{'r'};
  char_5 = 'f';
  char char_9{'r'};
  char_5 = 'w';
  char char_11{'g'};
  char_1 = 'j';
  char char_13{'o'};
  char_1 = 'w';
  char char_15{'m'};
  print("{}{}{}{}",
        char_3, char_13, char_7, char_15);
}

// Answer (4):

// __ __ __ __
```

**Puzzle 8**

```
void run() {
  char char_1{'j'};
  char char_2{'v'};
  char_2 = 'p';
  char char_4{'l'};
  char_1 = 'i';
  char char_6{'g'};
  char_2 = 'c';
  char char_8{'i'};
  char_8 = 'q';
```

```
  char char_10{'m'};
  char_1 = 'o';
  char char_12{'i'};
  char_1 = 't';
  char char_14{'e'};
  print("{}{}{}{}",
        char_2, char_14, char_12, char_4);
}

// Answer (4):

// __ __ __ __
```

# Copies

**Copy Example 1**

```
void run()
{
  int value = 4;
  auto copy = value;
  print("{}", copy);
}

// Answer: 4
```

**Copy Example 2**

```
void run()
{
  int value = 4;
  auto copy = value;
  copy = 7;
  print("{}", copy);
}

// Answer: 7
```

**Copy Example 3**

```
void run()
{
  int value = 4;
  auto copy = value;
  copy = 7;
  print("{}", value);
}

// Answer: 4
```

# char Copy Puzzles

**Puzzle 9**

```
void run() {
  char char_1{'a'};
  char_1 = 'R';
  char char_3{'u'};
  auto char_4 = char_1;
  char_3 = 'C';
  auto char_6 = char_4;
  char char_7{'i'};
  print("{}{}{}",
        char_6, char_3, char_4);
}

// Answer (3):

// __ __ __
```

**Puzzle 10**

```
void run() {
  char char_1{'a'};
  auto char_2 = char_1;
  char_2 = 'x';
  auto char_4 = char_1;
  char_1 = 'h';
  auto char_6 = char_1;
  char char_7{'e'};
  print("{}{}{}",
        char_1, char_7, char_2);
}

// Answer (3):

// __ __ __
```

**Puzzle 11**

```
void run() {
  char char_1{'v'};
  auto char_2 = char_1;
  char char_3{'s'};
  char_2 = 'm';
  char char_5{'d'};
  char_5 = 'b';
  auto char_7 = char_3;
  char char_8{'a'};
  print("{}{}{}",
        char_8, char_3, char_2);
}

// Answer (3):

// __ __ __
```

**Puzzle 12**

```
void run() {
  char char_1{'h'};
  char_1 = 'R';
  auto char_3 = char_1;
  char_3 = 'd';
  char char_5{'s'};
  char_5 = 'C';
  char char_7{'q'};
  char_7 = 'c';
  char char_9{'L'};
  char_3 = 'g';
  auto char_11 = char_5;
  print("{}{}{}",
        char_1, char_11, char_9);
}

// Answer (3):

// __ __ __
```

**Puzzle 13**

```
void run() {
  char char_1{'r'};
  char_1 = 'a';
  char char_3{'a'};
  char_1 = 'i';
  auto char_5 = char_1;
  char char_6{'n'};
  auto char_7 = char_1;
  char_1 = 'a';
  char char_9{'w'};
  auto char_10 = char_6;
  print("{}{}{}",
        char_10, char_3, char_6);
}

// Answer (3):

// __ __ __
```

**Puzzle 14**

```
void run() {
  char char_1{'o'};
  char_1 = 'u';
  auto char_3 = char_1;
  char_1 = 'p';
  char char_5{'t'};
  auto char_6 = char_1;
  char_1 = 'm';
  auto char_8 = char_6;
  char char_9{'l'};
  char_1 = 'o';
  auto char_11 = char_1;
  print("{}{}{}",
        char_1, char_3, char_5);
}

// Answer (3):

// __ __ __
```

**Puzzle 15**

```
void run() {
  char char_1{'l'};
  auto char_2 = char_1;
  char char_3{'e'};
  char_1 = 'q';
  char char_5{'y'};
  auto char_6 = char_2;
  char_5 = 'b';
  char char_8{'r'};
  auto char_9 = char_2;
  char_6 = 'p';
  auto char_11 = char_5;
  print("{}{}{}{}",
        char_2, char_3, char_8, char_6);
}

// Answer (4):

// __ __ __ __
```

**Puzzle 16**

```
void run() {
  char char_1{'f'};
  char_1 = 't';
  auto char_3 = char_1;
  char char_4{'o'};
  auto char_5 = char_4;
  char char_6{'g'};
  char_3 = 'u';
  char char_8{'v'};
  auto char_9 = char_4;
  char_3 = 'g';
  auto char_11 = char_8;
  print("{}{}{}{}",
        char_6, char_4, char_1, char_9);
}

// Answer (4):

// __ __ __ __
```

# References

**Reference Example 1**

```
void run()
{
  int value = 4;
  auto &reference = value;
  print("{}", reference);
}

// Answer: 4
```

**Reference Example 2**

```
void run()
{
  int value = 4;
  auto &reference = value;
  reference = 11;
  print("{}", reference);
}

// Answer: 11
```

**Reference Example 3**

```
void run()
{
  int value = 4;
  auto &reference = value;
  reference = 11;
  print("{}", value);
}

// Answer: 11
```

# char Reference Puzzles

**Puzzle 17**

```
void run() {
  char char_1{'u'};
  char_1 = 'h';
  auto &char_3 = char_1;
  char_1 = 'n';
  auto &char_5 = char_1;
  char_3 = 't';
  char char_7{'s'};
  char_5 = 'w';
  auto &char_9 = char_3;
  print("{}",
        char_5);
}

// Answer (1):

// __
```

**Puzzle 18**

```
void run() {
  char char_1{'y'};
  auto &char_2 = char_1;
  char char_3{'t'};
  char_1 = 'm';
  auto &char_5 = char_1;
  char char_6{'e'};
  print("{}{}",
        char_3, char_5);
}

// Answer (2):

// __ __
```

**Puzzle 19**

```
void run() {
  char char_1{'c'};
  char_1 = 't';
  auto &char_3 = char_1;
  char char_4{'e'};
  auto &char_5 = char_1;
  char char_6{'g'};
  auto &char_7 = char_4;
  print("{}{}{}",
        char_6, char_7, char_1);
}

// Answer (3):

// __ __ __
```

**Puzzle 20**

```
void run() {
  char char_1{'y'};
  char_1 = 'b';
  char char_3{'p'};
  char_3 = 'o';
  char char_5{'y'};
  auto &char_6 = char_5;
  char_6 = 'w';
  auto &char_8 = char_3;
  char char_9{'l'};
  print("{}{}{}{}",
        char_1, char_3, char_8, char_9);
}

// Answer (4):

// __ __ __ __
```

**Puzzle 21**

```
void run() {
  char char_1{'n'};
  char_1 = 'g';
  auto &char_3 = char_1;
  char char_4{'l'};
  auto &char_5 = char_4;
  char char_6{'c'};
  auto &char_7 = char_1;
  char_4 = 'd';
  auto &char_9 = char_3;
  print("{}{}{}",
        char_9, char_6, char_5);
}

// Answer (3):

// __ __ __
```

**Puzzle 22**

```
void run() {
  char char_1{'d'};
  char char_2{'i'};
  auto &char_3 = char_1;
  char char_4{'s'};
  char_3 = 'j';
  auto &char_6 = char_4;
  char char_7{'l'};
  auto &char_8 = char_6;
  print("{}{}",
        char_2, char_4);
}

// Answer (2):

// __ __
```

**Puzzle 23**

```
void run() {
  char char_1{'k'};
  auto &char_2 = char_1;
  char char_3{'k'};
  auto &char_4 = char_3;
  char char_5{'f'};
  char_5 = 'm';
  auto &char_7 = char_3;
  char_3 = 'a';
  char char_9{'g'};
  char_1 = 'm';
  auto &char_11 = char_2;
  print("{}{}{}{}{}",
        char_9, char_3, char_2, char_5, char_7);
}

// Answer (5):

// __ __ __ __ __
```

**Puzzle 24**

```
void run() {
  char char_1{'q'};
  auto &char_2 = char_1;
  char char_3{'f'};
  auto &char_4 = char_2;
  char char_5{'l'};
  char_3 = 'e';
  char char_7{'x'};
  char_3 = 'r';
  auto &char_9 = char_4;
  char_4 = 'o';
  char char_11{'l'};
  print("{}{}{}",
        char_7, char_1, char_3);
}

// Answer (3):

// __ __ __
```

**Puzzle 25**

```
void run() {
  char char_1{'A'};
  auto char_2 = char_1;
  char char_3{'w'};
  auto char_4 = char_1;
  auto &char_5 = char_2;
  char_4 = 'D';
  char char_7{'P'};
  print("{}{}",
        char_7, char_1);
  char char_8{'D'};
  auto &char_9 = char_8;
  auto char_10 = char_9;
  auto &char_11 = char_2;
  print("{}{}{}",
        char_4, char_10, char_9);
}

// Answer (5):

// __ __ __ __ __
```

**Puzzle 26**

```
void run() {
  char char_1{'g'};
  char_1 = 'f';
  print("{}",
        char_1);
  auto &char_3 = char_1;
  auto char_4 = char_1;
  auto &char_5 = char_4;
  char char_6{'v'};
  char_3 = 'h';
  auto char_8 = char_6;
  char_1 = 'o';
  auto &char_10 = char_1;
  char_6 = 'r';
  char char_12{'l'};
  auto char_13 = char_4;
  char_4 = 'l';
```

```
  char char_15{'y'};
  print("{}{}{}{}{}",
        char_5, char_10, char_3, char_6, char_4);
}

// Answer (6):

// __ __ __ __ __ __
```

**Puzzle 27**

```
void run() {
  char char_1{'q'};
  char_1 = 'f';
  auto char_3 = char_1;
  char char_4{'i'};
  auto &char_5 = char_4;
  char_4 = 'y';
  auto &char_7 = char_5;
  auto char_8 = char_5;
  auto &char_9 = char_8;
  char_5 = 'e';
  auto &char_11 = char_3;
  char_8 = 'k';
  char char_13{'s'};
  auto char_14 = char_9;
  print("{}{}{}{}{}",
        char_11, char_13, char_4, char_7, char_8);
}

// Answer (5):

// __ __ __ __ __
```

**Puzzle 28**

```
void run() {
  char char_1{'a'};
  char_1 = 'y';
  auto char_3 = char_1;
  auto &char_4 = char_1;
  char_1 = 'c';
  char char_6{'u'};
  auto char_7 = char_3;
  auto &char_8 = char_1;
  char char_9{'a'};
  char_7 = 'v';
  print("{}{}{}",
        char_8, char_9, char_6);
  auto char_11 = char_9;
  char char_12{'h'};
  auto char_13 = char_8;
  print("{}{}{}",
        char_13, char_12, char_3);
}

// Answer (6):

// __ __ __ __ __ __
```

**Puzzle 29**

```
void run() {
  char char_1{'t'};
  auto &char_2 = char_1;
  char char_3{'c'};
  auto char_4 = char_1;
  char_4 = 'g';
  char char_6{'l'};
  auto &char_7 = char_4;
  char char_8{'d'};
  char_8 = 'r';
  auto char_10 = char_3;
  char_7 = 'b';
  char char_12{'e'};
  auto char_13 = char_8;
  auto &char_14 = char_13;
```

```
  print("{}{}{}{}{}",
        char_3, char_4, char_8, char_1, char_6);
}

// Answer (5):

// __ __ __ __ __
```

**Puzzle 30**

```
void run() {
  char char_1{'e'};
  auto char_2 = char_1;
  char_1 = 'd';
  auto char_4 = char_1;
  char_4 = 'j';
  char char_6{'e'};
  print("{}{}",
        char_1, char_6);
  char_1 = 'w';
  auto &char_8 = char_4;
  char char_9{'l'};
  auto char_10 = char_6;
  auto &char_11 = char_2;
  char char_12{'t'};
  auto &char_13 = char_1;
  char char_14{'r'};
  print("{}{}{}{}",
        char_9, char_11, char_12, char_2);
}

// Answer (6):

// __ __ __ __ __ __
```

**Puzzle 31**

```
void run() {
  char char_1{'c'};
  auto char_2 = char_1;
  print("{}",
        char_1);
  auto &char_3 = char_2;
  char_2 = 'o';
  auto char_5 = char_3;
  char char_6{'n'};
  auto char_7 = char_2;
  char char_8{'m'};
  auto char_9 = char_5;
  auto &char_10 = char_8;
  char char_11{'n'};
  auto &char_12 = char_8;
  print("{}{}{}{}{}",
        char_9, char_10, char_12, char_5, char_11);
}

// Answer (6):

// __ __ __ __ __ __
```

**Puzzle 32**

```
void run() {
  char char_1{'H'};
  auto char_2 = char_1;
  char char_3{'D'};
  char_2 = 'A';
  auto &char_5 = char_2;
  auto char_6 = char_1;
  char char_7{'h'};
  auto char_8 = char_3;
  char_6 = 'D';
  char char_10{'P'};
  auto char_11 = char_2;
  char char_12{'i'};
  auto char_13 = char_1;
  print("{}{}{}{}{}{}",
        char_10, char_1, char_11, char_8, char_3, char_6);
```

```
}

// Answer (6):

// __ __ __ __ __ __
```

**Puzzle 33**

```
void run() {
  char char_1{'o'};
  char char_2{'f'};
  char_1 = 'i';
  auto &char_4 = char_2;
  auto char_5 = char_4;
  print("{}",
        char_4);
  char char_6{'p'};
  auto char_7 = char_5;
  auto &char_8 = char_2;
  auto char_9 = char_1;
  char_9 = 'm';
  auto &char_11 = char_6;
  auto char_12 = char_7;
  char char_13{'a'};
  print("{}{}{}",
        char_9, char_13, char_2);
}

// Answer (4):

// __ __ __ __
```

**Puzzle 34**

```
void run() {
  char char_1{'j'};
  char_1 = 's';
  auto char_3 = char_1;
  char char_4{'i'};
  char_1 = 'l';
  print("{}{}",
        char_4, char_3);
  char_4 = 'o';
```

```
  auto char_7 = char_3;
  char char_8{'x'};
  print("{}",
        char_1);
  char_4 = 't';
  auto char_10 = char_3;
  auto &char_11 = char_4;
  char_4 = 'e';
  char char_13{'b'};
  auto char_14 = char_8;
  auto &char_15 = char_7;
  char char_16{'t'};
  print("{}{}{}",
        char_11, char_10, char_15);
}

// Answer (6):

// __ __ __ __ __ __
```

**Puzzle 35**

```
void run() {
  char char_1{'H'};
  auto char_2 = char_1;
  auto &char_3 = char_1;
  auto char_4 = char_3;
  char_1 = 'y';
  auto &char_6 = char_1;
  auto char_7 = char_6;
  char char_8{'d'};
  char_8 = 'S';
  char char_10{'U'};
  char_1 = 'f';
  auto &char_12 = char_2;
  char_6 = 'A';
  char char_14{'P'};
  auto &char_15 = char_6;
  auto char_16 = char_10;
  print("{}{}{}{}{}",
        char_14, char_10, char_8, char_4, char_3);
}
```

```
// Answer (5):

// __ __ __ __ __
```

**Puzzle 36**

```
void run() {
  char char_1{'i'};
  char_1 = 's';
  auto &char_3 = char_1;
  char char_4{'k'};
  char_4 = 'k';
  auto char_6 = char_3;
  auto &char_7 = char_4;
  char_6 = 'j';
  auto char_9 = char_1;
  char char_10{'m'};
  char_1 = 'e';
  char char_12{'r'};
  char_10 = 'a';
  auto &char_14 = char_12;
  char_4 = 'p';
  auto &char_16 = char_4;
  char char_17{'g'};
  char_10 = 'o';
  char char_19{'r'};
  print("{}{}{}{}{}{}",
        char_16, char_1, char_14, char_19, char_10, char_12);
}

// Answer (6):

// __ __ __ __ __ __
```

**Puzzle 37**

```
void run() {
  char char_1{'x'};
  char_1 = 'f';
  char char_3{'l'};
  char_1 = 'l';
  auto &char_5 = char_1;
  char_3 = 'w';
  char char_7{'e'};
  char_5 = 'n';
  auto char_9 = char_7;
  char char_10{'p'};
  auto &char_11 = char_7;
  auto char_12 = char_5;
  char char_13{'c'};
  char_12 = 'x';
  char char_15{'t'};
  char_13 = 'g';
  auto char_17 = char_10;
  auto &char_18 = char_15;
  print("{}{}{}{}{}{}",
        char_9, char_12, char_15, char_11, char_1, char_18);
}

// Answer (6):

// __ __ __ __ __ __
```

**Puzzle 38**

```
void run() {
  char char_1{'l'};
  auto &char_2 = char_1;
  auto char_3 = char_1;
  print("{}{}",
        char_1, char_2);
  auto char_4 = char_2;
  char char_5{'s'};
  auto char_6 = char_2;
  char char_7{'d'};
  char_4 = 'x';
  char char_9{'_'};
```

```
  auto char_10 = char_9;
  char char_11{'t'};
  char_6 = 'v';
  char char_13{'i'};
  auto char_14 = char_9;
  print("{}{}{}{}{}",
        char_7, char_13, char_6, char_9, char_11);
}

// Answer (7):

// __ __ __ __ __ __ __
```

**Puzzle 39**

```
void run() {
  char char_1{'w'};
  auto &char_2 = char_1;
  auto char_3 = char_1;
  char_2 = 'f';
  auto &char_5 = char_2;
  auto char_6 = char_5;
  auto &char_7 = char_1;
  char_6 = 's';
  auto &char_9 = char_5;
  char_7 = 'c';
  auto &char_11 = char_1;
  print("{}{}{}",
        char_3, char_7, char_6);
  char char_12{'o'};
  auto &char_13 = char_7;
  char_5 = 'r';
  char char_15{'t'};
  auto &char_16 = char_6;
  print("{}{}{}",
        char_16, char_15, char_9);
}

// Answer (6):

// __ __ __ __ __ __
```

**Puzzle 40**

```
void run() {
  char char_1{'v'};
  char_1 = 'a';
  auto char_3 = char_1;
  char char_4{'b'};
  auto char_5 = char_1;
  char_1 = 'p';
  auto char_7 = char_5;
  char_5 = 'q';
  auto char_9 = char_4;
  char char_10{'e'};
  auto &char_11 = char_7;
  auto char_12 = char_4;
  char char_13{'t'};
  char_3 = 'e';
  auto char_15 = char_7;
  auto &char_16 = char_11;
  print("{}{}{}{}",
        char_9, char_3, char_13, char_15);
}

// Answer (4):

// __ __ __ __
```

**Puzzle 41**

```
void run() {
  char char_1{'m'};
  print("{}",
        char_1);
  char_1 = 'b';
  char char_3{'x'};
  char_3 = 'a';
  auto &char_5 = char_3;
  print("{}",
        char_3);
  char_3 = 'k';
  print("{}",
        char_5);
  char_3 = 'y';
```

```
  char char_8{'e'};
  print("{}",
        char_8);
  auto &char_9 = char_5;
  char char_10{'p'};
  char_8 = 'f';
  auto char_12 = char_3;
  char_3 = 'j';
  auto char_14 = char_3;
  char_14 = 'x';
  char char_16{'n'};
  char_14 = 'n';
  char char_18{'w'};
  char_14 = '_';
  auto char_20 = char_14;
  char char_21{'a'};
  char_18 = 'q';
  auto char_23 = char_5;
  print("{}{}{}{}",
        char_20, char_21, char_16, char_12);
}

// Answer (8):

// __ __ __ __ __ __ __ __
```

**Puzzle 42**

```
void run() {
  char char_1{'l'};
  auto &char_2 = char_1;
  print("{}",
        char_2);
  char_2 = 'n';
  auto &char_4 = char_1;
  char_1 = 'o';
  print("{}",
        char_4);
  char char_6{'2'};
  auto &char_7 = char_4;
  char char_8{'f'};
  char_1 = 'm';
  auto char_10 = char_2;
```

```
  char char_11{'g'};
  char_1 = 'r';
  char char_13{'f'};
  auto char_14 = char_13;
  char char_15{'l'};
  auto char_16 = char_11;
  auto &char_17 = char_15;
  print("{}{}{}",
        char_16, char_6, char_15);
}

// Answer (5):

// __ __ __ __ __
```

**Puzzle 43**

```
void run() {
  char char_1{'f'};
  auto &char_2 = char_1;
  print("{}",
        char_1);
  char char_3{'c'};
  char_3 = 'r';
  char char_5{'q'};
  char_5 = 'w';
  char char_7{'c'};
  char_2 = 'r';
  auto &char_9 = char_3;
  auto char_10 = char_7;
  auto &char_11 = char_10;
  char_9 = 'h';
  auto &char_13 = char_10;
  char_10 = 'r';
  char char_15{'o'};
  auto char_16 = char_11;
  char char_17{'e'};
  char_3 = 'o';
  auto &char_19 = char_10;
  print("{}{}{}{}{}",
        char_17, char_2, char_10, char_9, char_11);
}
```

```
// Answer (6):

// __ __ __ __ __ __
```

**Puzzle 44**

```
void run() {
  char char_1{'D'};
  char char_2{'u'};
  char_2 = 'K';
  auto char_4 = char_1;
  char char_5{'u'};
  auto char_6 = char_1;
  auto &char_7 = char_1;
  char char_8{'A'};
  auto char_9 = char_7;
  char_5 = 's';
  auto char_11 = char_8;
  char_6 = 'd';
  auto char_13 = char_4;
  auto &char_14 = char_1;
  char char_15{'h'};
  auto &char_16 = char_1;
  print("{}{}{}{}{}",
        char_2, char_8, char_16, char_14, char_4);
}

// Answer (5):

// __ __ __ __ __
```

**Puzzle 45**

```
void run() {
  char char_1{'n'};
  auto &char_2 = char_1;
  char char_3{'P'};
  char_1 = 'R';
  char char_5{'R'};
  auto &char_6 = char_1;
  print("{}{}",
        char_3, char_2);
  auto &char_7 = char_2;
```

```
  auto char_8 = char_2;
  char_8 = 'D';
  char char_10{'O'};
  auto char_11 = char_1;
  char_6 = 'V';
  char char_13{'m'};
  auto char_14 = char_10;
  char char_15{'b'};
  char_3 = 'w';
  auto char_17 = char_2;
  print("{}{}{}{}",
        char_10, char_5, char_7, char_8);
}

// Answer (6):

// __ __ __ __ __ __
```

**Puzzle 46**

```
void run() {
  char char_1{'j'};
  auto &char_2 = char_1;
  char_1 = 'd';
  char char_4{'b'};
  char_2 = 'l';
  char char_6{'c'};
  auto char_7 = char_6;
  print("{}{}",
        char_7, char_2);
  auto char_8 = char_7;
  auto &char_9 = char_8;
  char_6 = 'o';
  auto &char_11 = char_2;
  char char_12{'k'};
  auto char_13 = char_7;
  char_9 = '_';
  char char_15{'r'};
  char_1 = 't';
  auto &char_17 = char_8;
  auto char_18 = char_7;
  print("{}{}{}{}{}",
        char_6, char_18, char_12, char_8, char_11);
```

```
}

// Answer (7):

// __ __ __ __ __ __ __
```

**Puzzle 47**

```
void run() {
  char char_1{'o'};
  char_1 = 'w';
  auto &char_3 = char_1;
  char_3 = 'c';
  char char_5{'x'};
  auto &char_6 = char_5;
  auto char_7 = char_3;
  auto &char_8 = char_6;
  char char_9{'a'};
  auto &char_10 = char_9;
  auto char_11 = char_6;
  char_1 = 'f';
  char char_13{'n'};
  auto &char_14 = char_5;
  char_8 = 's';
  char char_16{'c'};
  auto &char_17 = char_14;
  char char_18{'v'};
  print("{}{}{}{}{}{}{}",
        char_18, char_17, char_14, char_7, char_10, char_13,
        char_1);
}

// Answer (7):

// __ __ __ __ __ __ __
```

**Puzzle 48**

```
void run() {
  char char_1{'D'};
  print("{}",
        char_1);
  char char_2{'r'};
  auto char_3 = char_2;
  auto &char_4 = char_3;
  auto char_5 = char_1;
  auto &char_6 = char_3;
  char char_7{'i'};
  char_3 = 'd';
  char char_9{'e'};
  char_5 = 'i';
  auto char_11 = char_3;
  char_7 = 'k';
  auto char_13 = char_5;
  char_2 = 'v';
  char char_15{'x'};
  auto &char_16 = char_13;
  char char_17{'m'};
  auto char_18 = char_15;
  print("{}{}{}{}{}",
        char_5, char_2, char_16, char_11, char_9);
}

// Answer (6):

// __ __ __ __ __ __
```

**Puzzle 49**

```
void run() {
  char char_1{'M'};
  print("{}",
        char_1);
  auto &char_2 = char_1;
  auto char_3 = char_1;
  char_2 = 'n';
  auto &char_5 = char_2;
  char char_6{'D'};
  auto char_7 = char_6;
```

```
  char char_8{'f'};
  auto char_9 = char_7;
  char_9 = 'x';
  auto char_11 = char_5;
  char char_12{'S'};
  auto &char_13 = char_9;
  char char_14{'v'};
  char_5 = 'V';
  char char_16{'X'};
  char_9 = 'O';
  auto char_18 = char_6;
  print("{}{}{}{}{}",
        char_9, char_2, char_12, char_16, char_18);
}

// Answer (6):

// __ __ __ __ __ __
```

**Puzzle 50**

```
void run() {
  char char_1{'u'};
  char char_2{'r'};
  auto &char_3 = char_2;
  char_3 = 'o';
  auto &char_5 = char_1;
  print("{}",
        char_3);
  char char_6{'t'};
  auto char_7 = char_5;
  auto &char_8 = char_3;
  char char_9{'_'};
  char_2 = 't';
  char char_11{'t'};
  auto &char_12 = char_8;
  auto char_13 = char_1;
  print("{}{}{}",
        char_13, char_12, char_9);
  char_1 = 'r';
  char char_15{'p'};
  auto char_16 = char_6;
  char_7 = 'e';
```

```
  char char_18{'_'};
  print("{}{}{}{}{}",
        char_15, char_8, char_5, char_18, char_11);
}

// Answer (9):

// __ __ __ __ __ __ __ __ __
```

**Puzzle 51**

```
void run() {
  char char_1{'r'};
  char_1 = 'i';
  auto char_3 = char_1;
  auto &char_4 = char_3;
  char char_5{'e'};
  auto char_6 = char_1;
  char char_7{'m'};
  char_6 = 'c';
  auto char_9 = char_4;
  char_1 = 'i';
  auto char_11 = char_1;
  char_11 = 'r';
  auto char_13 = char_5;
  auto &char_14 = char_13;
  auto char_15 = char_11;
  char char_16{'l'};
  char_4 = 'r';
  char char_18{'a'};
  auto &char_19 = char_3;
  print("{}{}{}{}{}{}{}{}",
        char_6, char_16, char_5, char_18, char_4, char_13,
        char_15, char_3);
}

// Answer (8):

// __ __ __ __ __ __ __ __
```

**Puzzle 52**

```
void run() {
  char char_1{'m'};
  auto char_2 = char_1;
  auto &char_3 = char_1;
  print("{}",
        char_3);
  char_2 = 'g';
  auto char_5 = char_1;
  char_5 = 'f';
  auto &char_7 = char_1;
  auto char_8 = char_3;
  char_5 = 'p';
  char char_10{'c'};
  auto &char_11 = char_2;
  auto char_12 = char_7;
  auto &char_13 = char_3;
  auto char_14 = char_5;
  char char_15{'q'};
  auto char_16 = char_7;
  char_11 = 'e';
  auto &char_18 = char_15;
  print("{}{}{}{}{}",
        char_2, char_1, char_10, char_8, char_14);
}

// Answer (6):

// __ __ __ __ __ __
```

**Puzzle 53**

```
void run() {
  char char_1{'r'};
  auto char_2 = char_1;
  auto &char_3 = char_1;
  auto char_4 = char_1;
  char_3 = 'r';
  char char_6{'p'};
  auto char_7 = char_3;
  char char_8{'o'};
  auto char_9 = char_4;
```

```
  auto &char_10 = char_6;
  char char_11{'p'};
  auto &char_12 = char_10;
  char_9 = 't';
  auto char_14 = char_8;
  char_11 = 'e';
  auto &char_16 = char_3;
  auto char_17 = char_4;
  char char_18{'g'};
  print("{}{}{}{}{}",
        char_11, char_4, char_1, char_14, char_2);
}

// Answer (5):

// __ __ __ __ __
```

**Puzzle 54**

```
void run() {
  char char_1{'p'};
  auto char_2 = char_1;
  auto &char_3 = char_2;
  char_3 = 'h';
  char char_5{'u'};
  auto &char_6 = char_5;
  char char_7{'y'};
  auto char_8 = char_1;
  char_6 = 'r';
  char char_10{'o'};
  auto &char_11 = char_3;
  char char_12{'m'};
  char_12 = 'i';
  auto &char_14 = char_7;
  char_8 = 'b';
  auto &char_16 = char_5;
  auto char_17 = char_12;
  char_8 = 'h';
  auto &char_19 = char_8;
  char_8 = 'm';
  char char_21{'t'};
  print("{}{}{}{}{}{}",
        char_12, char_19, char_1, char_10, char_16, char_21);
```

```
}

// Answer (6):

// __ __ __ __ __ __
```

**Puzzle 55**

```
void run() {
  char char_1{'a'};
  auto char_2 = char_1;
  char char_3{'r'};
  auto &char_4 = char_2;
  auto char_5 = char_4;
  char_1 = 'c';
  char char_7{'e'};
  auto char_8 = char_7;
  char_4 = 'm';
  print("{}{}{}",
        char_4, char_8, char_3);
  char char_10{'l'};
  auto &char_11 = char_2;
  char_4 = 'b';
  char char_13{'g'};
  auto &char_14 = char_10;
  auto char_15 = char_3;
  auto &char_16 = char_8;
  char char_17{'l'};
  auto &char_18 = char_15;
  print("{}{}{}{}{}{}",
        char_13, char_16, char_5, char_2, char_17, char_7);
}

// Answer (9):

// __ __ __ __ __ __ __ __ __
```

**Puzzle 56**

```
void run() {
  char char_1{'s'};
  auto char_2 = char_1;
  auto &char_3 = char_1;
  auto char_4 = char_1;
  auto &char_5 = char_1;
  char_1 = 'i';
  auto char_7 = char_2;
  char_4 = 'h';
  char char_9{'m'};
  auto &char_10 = char_2;
  char char_11{'g'};
  auto &char_12 = char_5;
  auto char_13 = char_4;
  char char_14{'t'};
  auto char_15 = char_10;
  char_9 = 'w';
  char char_17{'x'};
  char_10 = 'd';
  auto &char_19 = char_14;
  print("{}{}{}{}{}{}{}{}{}",
        char_5, char_15, char_9, char_17, char_2, char_3,
        char_11, char_1, char_19);
}

// Answer (9):

// __ __ __ __ __ __ __ __ __
```

# Functions

#### Function Example 1

```
void update_copy(int parameter) {
  parameter = 5;
}

void run()
{
  int value = 7;
  update_copy(value);
  fmt::print("{}", value);
}

// Answer: 7
```

#### Function Example 2

```
void update_reference(int &parameter) {
  parameter = 5;
}

void run()
{
  int value = 7;
  update_reference(value);
  fmt::print("{}", value);
}

// Answer: 5
```

# char Puzzles With Functions

**Puzzle 57**

```
auto function(char parameter_1, char &parameter_2) {
  char char_1{'s'};
  auto char_2 = parameter_1;
  char_1 = 'r';
  char char_4{'a'};
  auto char_5 = char_1;
  parameter_2 = 'm';
  print("{}{}",
        parameter_1, char_1);
}
void run() {
  char char_1{'s'};
  auto char_2 = char_1;
  char char_3{'r'};
  char_3 = 'a';
  auto char_5 = char_2;
  char_2 = 'm';
  char char_7{'r'};
  print("{}",
        char_5);
  auto char_8 = char_7;
  auto &char_9 = char_7;
  char_8 = 'i';
  auto &char_11 = char_5;
  char char_12{'t'};
  print("{}{}{}",
        char_12, char_7, char_1);
  function(char_12, char_11);
  char_7 = 'e';
  auto char_14 = char_5;
  print("{}{}{}",
        char_9, char_3, char_14);
}

// Answer (9):

// __ __ __ __ __ __ __ __ __
```

**Puzzle 58**

```
auto function(char &parameter_1, char &parameter_2) {
  char char_1{'s'};
  parameter_1 = 'a';
  print("{}",
        char_1);
  char char_3{'m'};
  auto char_4 = char_3;
  print("{}{}",
        parameter_1, char_3);
}
void run() {
  char char_1{'s'};
  char char_2{'a'};
  function(char_1, char_2);
  char_2 = 'm';
  auto &char_4 = char_2;
  char char_5{'l'};
  auto &char_6 = char_2;
  char char_7{'p'};
  auto char_8 = char_5;
  char_2 = 'e';
  char char_10{'l'};
  auto &char_11 = char_4;
  auto char_12 = char_6;
  print("{}{}{}",
        char_7, char_5, char_6);
}

// Answer (6):

// __ __ __ __ __ __
```

**Puzzle 59**

```
auto function(char &parameter_1, char &parameter_2) {
  parameter_2 = 'a';
  parameter_1 = 'o';
  print("{}",
        parameter_2);
  char char_3{'m'};
  auto &char_4 = parameter_2;
  parameter_2 = 'c';
  print("{}{}",
        char_4, parameter_1);
}
void run() {
  char char_1{'a'};
  auto char_2 = char_1;
  char_2 = 'k';
  char char_4{'f'};
  char_4 = 'c';
  char char_6{'s'};
  function(char_4, char_1);
  char_1 = 'e';
  auto char_8 = char_2;
  char_8 = 'l';
  auto char_10 = char_1;
  char_2 = 'g';
  auto char_12 = char_4;
  auto &char_13 = char_6;
  char char_14{'x'};
  auto char_15 = char_10;
  char char_16{'h'};
  print("{}{}{}",
        char_13, char_16, char_8);
}

// Answer (6):

// __ __ __ __ __ __
```

**Puzzle 60**

```
auto function(char &parameter_1, char &parameter_2) {
  char char_1{'m'};
  char_1 = 'n';
  auto &char_3 = char_1;
  auto char_4 = parameter_2;
  char_4 = 'e';
  auto char_6 = char_4;
  print("{}{}",
        parameter_1, char_6);
}
void run() {
  char char_1{'m'};
  char char_2{'n'};
  function(char_1, char_2);
  auto &char_3 = char_2;
  auto char_4 = char_3;
  char_1 = 'e';
  char char_6{'r'};
  char_1 = 'u';
  print("{}",
        char_6);
  char_3 = 'x';
  auto &char_9 = char_1;
  char char_10{'s'};
  char_9 = 'e';
  char char_12{'n'};
  auto &char_13 = char_1;
  auto char_14 = char_3;
  function(char_10, char_9);
  auto char_15 = char_6;
  print("{}{}{}",
        char_4, char_12, char_13);
}

// Answer (8):

// __ __ __ __ __ __ __ __
```

**Puzzle 61**

```
auto function(char parameter_1, char &parameter_2) {
  print("{}",
        parameter_1);
  parameter_1 = 'p';
  char char_2{'t'};
  auto char_3 = char_2;
  parameter_2 = 'l';
  auto &char_5 = char_3;
  print("{}",
        char_5);
}
void run() {
  char char_1{'x'};
  auto char_2 = char_1;
  char char_3{'s'};
  auto char_4 = char_2;
  char_4 = 'q';
  function(char_3, char_4);
  auto &char_6 = char_4;
  auto char_7 = char_2;
  char char_8{'a'};
  auto char_9 = char_3;
  char_2 = 'o';
  auto char_11 = char_3;
  auto &char_12 = char_9;
  char_1 = 's';
  auto char_14 = char_6;
  print("{}{}{}",
        char_2, char_4, char_6);
}

// Answer (5):

// __ __ __ __ __
```

**Puzzle 62**

```
auto function(char &parameter_1, char &parameter_2) {
  char char_1{'j'};
  print("{}",
        parameter_2);
  auto char_2 = parameter_1;
  char_1 = 'C';
  auto &char_4 = char_2;
  char_1 = 'a';
  print("{}",
        parameter_1);
}
void run() {
  char char_1{'j'};
  auto char_2 = char_1;
  char_1 = 'C';
  char char_4{'a'};
  auto &char_5 = char_4;
  char_2 = 'l';
  function(char_5, char_1);
  auto &char_7 = char_5;
  char char_8{'b'};
  auto char_9 = char_2;
  char char_10{'g'};
  auto char_11 = char_7;
  char_1 = 'e';
  char char_13{'l'};
  auto char_14 = char_9;
  print("{}{}{}{}{}{}",
        char_2, char_13, char_4, char_8, char_14, char_1);
}

// Answer (8):

// __ __ __ __ __ __ __ __
```

**Puzzle 63**

```
auto function(char parameter_1, char &parameter_2) {
  parameter_1 = 'l';
  char char_2{'D'};
  char_2 = 'L';
  auto &char_4 = char_2;
  parameter_1 = 'm';
  char char_6{'i'};
  print("{}",
        char_2);
}
void run() {
  char char_1{'l'};
  char_1 = 'D';
  auto char_3 = char_1;
  char char_4{'q'};
  auto &char_5 = char_1;
  auto char_6 = char_4;
  char char_7{'n'};
  auto &char_8 = char_7;
  char char_9{'w'};
  auto &char_10 = char_3;
  char_8 = 't';
  char char_12{'S'};
  char_3 = 'p';
  char char_14{'O'};
  function(char_4, char_6);
  char char_15{'w'};
  print("{}{}{}{}",
        char_14, char_1, char_12, char_5);
}

// Answer (5):

// __ __ __ __ __
```

**Puzzle 64**

```
auto function(char &parameter_1, char parameter_2) {
  print("{}",
        parameter_1);
  parameter_1 = 's';
  char char_2{'x'};
  parameter_2 = 'p';
  auto char_4 = char_2;
  char_4 = 'a';
  print("{}",
        char_4);
}
void run() {
  char char_1{'p'};
  auto &char_2 = char_1;
  char_1 = 'p';
  auto &char_4 = char_1;
  function(char_4, char_1);
  char_2 = 'a';
  auto char_6 = char_1;
  char char_7{'r'};
  auto &char_8 = char_6;
  char char_9{'d'};
  auto &char_10 = char_1;
  char_7 = 'k';
  char char_12{'h'};
  char_4 = 'g';
  char char_14{'c'};
  auto char_15 = char_12;
  char char_16{'e'};
  print("{}{}{}{}{}{}",
        char_14, char_7, char_8, char_1, char_16, char_9);
}

// Answer (8):

// __ __ __ __ __ __ __ __
```

**Puzzle 65**

```
auto function(char &parameter_1, char parameter_2) {
  parameter_1 = 'c';
  char char_2{'.'};
  parameter_1 = 'm';
  auto &char_4 = char_2;
  char char_5{'k'};
  auto char_6 = parameter_1;
  print("{}{}",
        char_4, parameter_2);
}
void run() {
  char char_1{'c'};
  char char_2{'.'};
  auto &char_3 = char_2;
  char_3 = 'b';
  auto char_5 = char_2;
  char_2 = 'p';
  auto char_7 = char_3;
  auto &char_8 = char_3;
  auto char_9 = char_2;
  print("{}{}{}",
        char_1, char_9, char_7);
  char_8 = 's';
  auto char_11 = char_8;
  function(char_7, char_8);
  char_2 = 'u';
  auto &char_13 = char_3;
  auto char_14 = char_7;
  char char_15{'j'};
  char_1 = 'x';
  char char_17{'t'};
  print("{}{}{}{}",
        char_3, char_5, char_11, char_17);
}

// Answer (9):

// __ __ __ __ __ __ __ __ __
```

**Puzzle 66**

```
auto function(char parameter_1, char &parameter_2) {
  parameter_1 = 'W';
  parameter_1 = 's';
  print("{}",
        parameter_2);
  parameter_1 = 'x';
  char char_4{'C'};
  auto &char_5 = char_4;
  print("{}",
        char_4);
}
void run() {
  char char_1{'W'};
  char char_2{'k'};
  auto char_3 = char_1;
  auto &char_4 = char_2;
  char_3 = 'Q';
  auto char_6 = char_1;
  auto &char_7 = char_1;
  char_6 = 'c';
  char char_9{'q'};
  auto &char_10 = char_9;
  char_10 = 'P';
  char char_12{'E'};
  function(char_12, char_10);
  char_2 = 'M';
  char char_14{'e'};
  auto &char_15 = char_6;
  auto char_16 = char_7;
  print("{}{}{}{}{}",
        char_4, char_9, char_12, char_3, char_1);
}

// Answer (7):

// __ __ __ __ __ __ __
```

**Puzzle 67**

```
auto function(char &parameter_1, char &parameter_2) {
  print("{}",
        parameter_2);
  print("{}",
        parameter_1);
  parameter_1 = 'a';
  parameter_1 = 'a';
  char char_3{'r'};
  print("{}",
        char_3);
}
void run() {
  char char_1{'u'};
  auto char_2 = char_1;
  char char_3{'r'};
  char_3 = 'r';
  auto &char_5 = char_3;
  char_5 = 'v';
  auto char_7 = char_5;
  char char_8{'a'};
  char_3 = 't';
  auto &char_10 = char_2;
  char_2 = 'i';
  char char_12{'i'};
  auto char_13 = char_1;
  char char_14{'y'};
  char_13 = 'e';
  function(char_8, char_7);
  char char_16{'n'};
  auto char_17 = char_8;
  char char_18{'a'};
  print("{}{}{}{}",
        char_2, char_8, char_16, char_5);
}

// Answer (7):

// __ __ __ __ __ __ __
```

**Puzzle 68**

```
auto function(char &parameter_1, char parameter_2) {
  parameter_1 = ':';
  char char_2{'y'};
  auto &char_3 = parameter_1;
  auto char_4 = parameter_2;
  char char_5{'a'};
  auto char_6 = char_3;
  print("{}{}{}{}",
        char_5, char_2, parameter_1, char_3);
}
void run() {
  char char_1{':'};
  auto &char_2 = char_1;
  char char_3{'a'};
  char_3 = 'm';
  char char_5{'a'};
  char_3 = 'f';
  char char_7{'r'};
  print("{}{}",
        char_5, char_7);
  char_1 = 'r';
  print("{}",
        char_1);
  auto &char_9 = char_1;
  char_9 = 'y';
  auto &char_11 = char_7;
  char_1 = 'r';
  char char_13{'l'};
  auto &char_14 = char_2;
  char char_15{'m'};
  function(char_2, char_1);
  char_15 = 'i';
  char char_17{'a'};
  auto char_18 = char_13;
  char_13 = 'l';
  char char_20{'m'};
  print("{}{}{}{}",
        char_3, char_15, char_13, char_18);
}

// Answer (11):
```

```
// __ __ __ __ __ __ __ __ __ __ __
```

**Puzzle 69**

```
auto function(char &parameter_1, char &parameter_2) {
  parameter_1 = 'P';
  char char_2{'S'};
  parameter_2 = 'U';
  auto char_4 = parameter_1;
  char char_5{'b'};
  auto &char_6 = parameter_1;
  print("{}{}",
        char_2, char_6);
}
void run() {
  char char_1{'P'};
  print("{}",
        char_1);
  auto &char_2 = char_1;
  function(char_1, char_2);
  char char_3{'U'};
  auto char_4 = char_1;
  auto &char_5 = char_4;
  char_4 = 'B';
  auto char_7 = char_2;
  char_3 = 'i';
  char char_9{'U'};
  auto char_10 = char_1;
  char char_11{'h'};
  char_10 = 'q';
  char char_13{'d'};
  auto char_14 = char_7;
  auto &char_15 = char_11;
  char char_16{'S'};
  print("{}{}{}{}",
        char_5, char_9, char_16, char_4);
}

// Answer (7):

// __ __ __ __ __ __ __
```

**Puzzle 70**

```
auto function(char &parameter_1, char parameter_2) {
  parameter_2 = 'e';
  char char_2{'t'};
  parameter_2 = 'x';
  char char_4{'d'};
  parameter_1 = 'g';
  auto char_6 = parameter_2;
  print("{}",
        char_2);
}
void run() {
  char char_1{'j'};
  auto char_2 = char_1;
  auto &char_3 = char_1;
  char char_4{'o'};
  auto &char_5 = char_1;
  char char_6{'q'};
  auto &char_7 = char_3;
  function(char_7, char_5);
  char char_8{'a'};
  print("{}{}",
        char_3, char_8);
  char_4 = 'a';
  char char_10{'i'};
  char_3 = 'i';
  char char_12{'a'};
  auto &char_13 = char_10;
  char char_14{'e'};
  char_3 = 'm';
  auto &char_16 = char_8;
  print("{}{}{}",
        char_1, char_5, char_12);
}

// Answer (6):

// __ __ __ __ __ __
```

**Puzzle 71**

```
auto function(char &parameter_1, char parameter_2) {
  char char_1{'i'};
  auto &char_2 = char_1;
  char_1 = 's';
  print("{}{}",
        parameter_1, parameter_2);
  char char_4{'x'};
  auto char_5 = char_1;
  print("{}{}",
        char_1, char_2);
}
void run() {
  char char_1{'i'};
  auto &char_2 = char_1;
  char char_3{'s'};
  auto &char_4 = char_2;
  print("{}{}",
        char_2, char_3);
  char char_5{'e'};
  char_1 = 'q';
  auto &char_7 = char_4;
  char char_8{'u'};
  auto &char_9 = char_5;
  auto char_10 = char_4;
  auto &char_11 = char_9;
  char_4 = 'l';
  function(char_4, char_9);
  auto char_13 = char_1;
  char_2 = 'p';
  auto &char_15 = char_1;
  char char_16{'j'};
  char_7 = 'l';
  char char_18{'a'};
  print("{}{}{}{}{}",
        char_11, char_10, char_8, char_18, char_15);
}

// Answer (11):

// __ __ __ __ __ __ __ __ __ __ __
```

**Puzzle 72**

```
auto function(char &parameter_1, char parameter_2) {
  char char_1{'d'};
  auto &char_2 = parameter_1;
  auto char_3 = parameter_2;
  auto &char_4 = parameter_2;
  auto char_5 = parameter_1;
  char_1 = 'i';
  print("{}{}",
        char_3, char_1);
}
void run() {
  char char_1{'y'};
  char_1 = 's';
  char char_3{'r'};
  auto char_4 = char_3;
  print("{}",
        char_1);
  char_3 = 'c';
  auto char_6 = char_3;
  char char_7{'o'};
  char_7 = 'i';
  char char_9{'c'};
  char_1 = 't';
  auto &char_11 = char_7;
  char_6 = 'e';
  auto char_13 = char_1;
  char char_14{'o'};
  auto &char_15 = char_7;
  function(char_4, char_9);
  char char_16{'n'};
  auto char_17 = char_11;
  char char_18{'f'};
  auto char_19 = char_6;
  print("{}{}{}{}{}{}{}",
        char_6, char_16, char_13, char_17, char_18, char_7,
        char_3);
}

// Answer (10):

// __ __ __ __ __ __ __ __ __ __
```

**Puzzle 73**

```
auto function(char &parameter_1, char parameter_2) {
  char char_1{'o'};
  auto char_2 = parameter_1;
  parameter_2 = 's';
  auto char_4 = parameter_2;
  char char_5{'t'};
  char_1 = 'c';
  print("{}{}{}",
        char_4, char_5, parameter_1);
}
void run() {
  char char_1{'o'};
  auto &char_2 = char_1;
  auto char_3 = char_1;
  char char_4{'l'};
  auto &char_5 = char_4;
  char char_6{'c'};
  auto char_7 = char_4;
  auto &char_8 = char_1;
  char char_9{'r'};
  auto char_10 = char_4;
  function(char_9, char_2);
  char char_11{'u'};
  auto char_12 = char_5;
  char char_13{'w'};
  auto &char_14 = char_2;
  print("{}{}{}{}",
        char_6, char_2, char_7, char_5);
}

// Answer (7):

// __ __ __ __ __ __ __
```

**Puzzle 74**

```
auto function(char parameter_1, char &parameter_2) {
  char char_1{'o'};
  char char_2{'c'};
  auto char_3 = char_1;
  char_3 = 'o';
  auto &char_5 = char_3;
  auto char_6 = parameter_1;
  print("{}{}{}",
        char_1, parameter_1, char_2);
}
void run() {
  char char_1{'o'};
  char_1 = 'c';
  print("{}",
        char_1);
  auto &char_3 = char_1;
  char char_4{'w'};
  auto &char_5 = char_3;
  auto char_6 = char_5;
  char_4 = 'e';
  auto char_8 = char_3;
  char char_9{'t'};
  char_8 = 'e';
  auto char_11 = char_9;
  auto &char_12 = char_11;
  char char_13{'n'};
  auto char_14 = char_11;
  auto &char_15 = char_11;
  auto char_16 = char_13;
  function(char_13, char_8);
  char_3 = 's';
  char char_18{'p'};
  print("{}{}{}{}",
        char_4, char_18, char_14, char_3);
}

// Answer (8):

// __ __ __ __ __ __ __ __
```

**Puzzle 75**

```
auto function(char &parameter_1, char &parameter_2) {
  parameter_2 = 'r';
  parameter_1 = 'd';
  char char_3{'n'};
  auto char_4 = parameter_1;
  char char_5{'.'};
  auto &char_6 = char_5;
  print("{}{}{}",
        char_3, char_4, char_6);
}
void run() {
  char char_1{'r'};
  print("{}",
        char_1);
  char_1 = 'd';
  auto &char_3 = char_1;
  char_1 = 'a';
  auto char_5 = char_3;
  print("{}",
        char_3);
  auto char_6 = char_5;
  char char_7{'t'};
  function(char_3, char_1);
  char char_8{'l'};
  auto char_9 = char_8;
  auto &char_10 = char_7;
  auto char_11 = char_3;
  char char_12{'n'};
  char_10 = 'e';
  char char_14{'g'};
  char_14 = 'r';
  auto char_16 = char_7;
  char char_17{'g'};
  print("{}{}{}{}{}",
        char_17, char_10, char_12, char_7, char_14);
  char char_18{'s'};
  auto char_19 = char_9;
  print("{}{}",
        char_6, char_9);
}
```

```
// Answer (12):

// __ __ __ __ __ __ __ __ __ __ __ __
```

**Puzzle 76**

```
auto function(char parameter_1, char &parameter_2) {
  parameter_2 = 'd';
  char char_2{'c'};
  auto char_3 = char_2;
  char_3 = 'i';
  char char_5{'x'};
  char_3 = 'n';
  print("{}{}",
        parameter_2, char_2);
}
void run() {
  char char_1{'d'};
  char_1 = 'c';
  auto &char_3 = char_1;
  auto char_4 = char_3;
  char char_5{'f'};
  function(char_5, char_1);
  char char_6{'n'};
  auto char_7 = char_5;
  char char_8{'.'};
  char_3 = 'i';
  char char_10{'l'};
  print("{}{}{}{}",
        char_10, char_8, char_1, char_6);
  char_8 = 's';
  char char_12{'t'};
  auto char_13 = char_8;
  char char_14{'t'};
  char_7 = 'i';
  auto &char_16 = char_7;
  char_14 = '.';
  char char_18{'l'};
  auto char_19 = char_12;
  char char_20{'i'};
  print("{}{}{}{}{}{}{}",
        char_7, char_12, char_14, char_18, char_3, char_13,
        char_19);
```

```
}

// Answer (13):

// __ __ __ __ __ __ __ __ __ __ __ __ __
```

**Puzzle 77**

```
auto function(char &parameter_1, char &parameter_2) {
  char char_1{'t'};
  parameter_1 = 'i';
  char char_3{'r'};
  auto &char_4 = char_1;
  print("{}",
        char_1);
  auto &char_5 = char_3;
  print("{}",
        char_5);
}
void run() {
  char char_1{'t'};
  char_1 = 'i';
  auto &char_3 = char_1;
  char char_4{'n'};
  print("{}{}",
        char_1, char_4);
  char_3 = 'p';
  char char_6{'u'};
  char_4 = 'y';
  function(char_6, char_4);
  char_4 = 'v';
  char char_9{'o'};
  auto &char_10 = char_9;
  auto char_11 = char_1;
  char char_12{'s'};
  auto &char_13 = char_10;
  char_1 = 'l';
  auto &char_15 = char_11;
  auto char_16 = char_9;
  char_3 = 'c';
  char char_18{'e'};
  auto &char_19 = char_11;
  auto char_20 = char_1;
```

```
  char char_21{'.'};
  print("{}{}{}{}{}{}{}",
        char_9, char_21, char_12, char_20, char_10, char_11,
        char_18);
}

// Answer (11):

// __ __ __ __ __ __ __ __ __ __ __
```

**Puzzle 78**

```
auto function(char &parameter_1, char &parameter_2) {
  parameter_1 = 'y';
  parameter_1 = 'h';
  char char_3{'u'};
  parameter_1 = 'e';
  char char_5{'j'};
  char_5 = 't';
  print("{}{}",
        char_5, parameter_1);
}
void run() {
  char char_1{'y'};
  auto &char_2 = char_1;
  auto char_3 = char_1;
  char char_4{'e'};
  auto char_5 = char_2;
  auto &char_6 = char_5;
  char_5 = 'w';
  char char_8{'.'};
  auto &char_9 = char_2;
  char_5 = 'p';
  function(char_1, char_3);
  auto &char_11 = char_6;
  char char_12{'n'};
  auto char_13 = char_9;
  auto &char_14 = char_12;
  char char_15{'t'};
  auto char_16 = char_8;
  char_4 = 'm';
  auto &char_18 = char_3;
  print("{}{}{}{}{}{}{}",
```

```
        char_4, char_6, char_8, char_15, char_18, char_5,
        char_1);
}

// Answer (9):

// __ __ __ __ __ __ __ __ __
```

**Puzzle 79**

```
auto function(char parameter_1, char &parameter_2) {
  print("{}",
        parameter_1);
  char char_1{'.'};
  auto char_2 = parameter_2;
  char_2 = 'r';
  auto char_4 = parameter_2;
  char_4 = 'g';
  print("{}",
        char_2);
}
void run() {
  char char_1{'.'};
  auto char_2 = char_1;
  char_1 = 'r';
  char char_4{'e'};
  print("{}{}",
        char_1, char_4);
  char char_5{'g'};
  auto &char_6 = char_4;
  char_6 = 't';
  auto char_8 = char_6;
  function(char_2, char_1);
  auto &char_9 = char_1;
  char_1 = 'i';
  char char_11{'o'};
  auto char_12 = char_1;
  char char_13{'r'};
  auto char_14 = char_4;
  char_9 = 'e';
  char char_16{'r'};
  auto &char_17 = char_4;
  char_2 = 'm';
```

```
  auto char_19 = char_11;
  auto &char_20 = char_14;
  char char_21{'e'};
  print("{}{}{}{}{}{}",
        char_21, char_5, char_12, char_14, char_9, char_13);
}

// Answer (10):

// __ __ __ __ __ __ __ __ __ __
```

**Puzzle 80**

```
auto function(char &parameter_1, char &parameter_2) {
  parameter_1 = 'i';
  parameter_2 = 'n';
  char char_3{'z'};
  auto &char_4 = char_3;
  parameter_1 = 's';
  char char_6{'.'};
  print("{}{}",
        char_6, parameter_2);
}
void run() {
  char char_1{'i'};
  auto char_2 = char_1;
  char char_3{'z'};
  auto &char_4 = char_2;
  auto char_5 = char_4;
  auto &char_6 = char_1;
  char char_7{'e'};
  auto char_8 = char_1;
  char char_9{'m'};
  char_4 = 'e';
  auto &char_11 = char_8;
  char_5 = 'b';
  auto char_13 = char_4;
  char char_14{'i'};
  auto char_15 = char_5;
  char_8 = 'o';
  print("{}{}{}{}{}{}",
        char_3, char_11, char_9, char_15, char_1, char_2);
  char_14 = 'a';
```

```
  function(char_11, char_15);
  auto &char_18 = char_9;
  auto char_19 = char_9;
  auto &char_20 = char_9;
  print("{}{}{}{}",
        char_14, char_19, char_4, char_8);
}

// Answer (12):

// __ __ __ __ __ __ __ __ __ __ __ __
```

**Puzzle 81**

```
auto function(char &parameter_1, char parameter_2) {
  char char_1{'P'};
  char char_2{'G'};
  auto char_3 = parameter_1;
  char_3 = 'A';
  char char_5{'V'};
  auto &char_6 = char_3;
  print("{}{}{}{}",
        char_5, parameter_1, char_2, char_6);
}
void run() {
  char char_1{'P'};
  auto &char_2 = char_1;
  function(char_2, char_1);
  auto char_3 = char_2;
  char_3 = 'A';
  auto char_5 = char_3;
  char_2 = 'b';
  char char_7{'T'};
  auto char_8 = char_1;
  char_8 = 'o';
  auto &char_10 = char_3;
  char char_11{'m'};
  auto char_12 = char_8;
  char_11 = 'H';
  auto &char_14 = char_1;
  char_8 = 'R';
  char char_16{'n'};
  char_10 = 'w';
```

```
  char char_18{'Q'};
  auto char_19 = char_8;
  auto &char_20 = char_8;
  auto char_21 = char_18;
  char char_22{'E'};
  print("{}{}{}{}{}{}",
        char_7, char_11, char_22, char_19, char_21, char_18);
}

// Answer (10):

// __ __ __ __ __ __ __ __ __ __
```

**Puzzle 82**

```
auto function(char parameter_1, char &parameter_2) {
  parameter_1 = 'd';
  parameter_1 = 'o';
  print("{}",
        parameter_2);
  parameter_2 = 'o';
  print("{}",
        parameter_1);
  parameter_2 = 'd';
}
void run() {
  char char_1{'f'};
  char_1 = 'o';
  auto char_3 = char_1;
  auto &char_4 = char_3;
  char char_5{'c'};
  char_4 = 'a';
  auto char_7 = char_3;
  function(char_1, char_5);
  auto char_8 = char_1;
  char char_9{'o'};
  auto char_10 = char_7;
  char_10 = 'i';
  auto char_12 = char_5;
  char_5 = 'w';
  auto char_14 = char_10;
  auto &char_15 = char_8;
  char_12 = '_';
```

```
  auto char_17 = char_7;
  char char_18{'i'};
  auto &char_19 = char_14;
  auto char_20 = char_3;
  char char_21{'t'};
  print("{}{}{}{}{}{}",
        char_12, char_4, char_5, char_3, char_10, char_21);
}

// Answer (8):

// __ __ __ __ __ __ __ __
```

**Puzzle 83**

```
auto function(char parameter_1, char &parameter_2) {
  char char_1{'i'};
  print("{}{}",
        parameter_2, char_1);
  char char_2{'t'};
  auto char_3 = parameter_1;
  auto &char_4 = parameter_1;
  auto char_5 = parameter_1;
  print("{}{}",
        char_5, char_3);
}
void run() {
  char char_1{'i'};
  char_1 = 'h';
  char char_3{'x'};
  char_1 = 'n';
  auto &char_5 = char_3;
  auto char_6 = char_1;
  char char_7{'d'};
  char_3 = 'f';
  auto char_9 = char_1;
  char char_10{'o'};
  auto &char_11 = char_10;
  char char_12{'u'};
  auto &char_13 = char_12;
  char char_14{'q'};
  char_14 = 'f';
  auto &char_16 = char_1;
```

```
  char char_17{'u'};
  auto &char_18 = char_17;
  char char_19{'w'};
  char_3 = '.';
  auto char_21 = char_9;
  function(char_14, char_7);
  char_10 = 'l';
  auto &char_23 = char_11;
  print("{}{}{}{}{}",
        char_3, char_6, char_13, char_10, char_23);
}

// Answer (9):

// __ __ __ __ __ __ __ __ __
```

**Puzzle 84**

```
auto function(char &parameter_1, char &parameter_2) {
  parameter_1 = 'h';
  parameter_1 = 'l';
  char char_3{'o'};
  char_3 = 'e';
  auto &char_5 = parameter_2;
  auto char_6 = parameter_2;
  print("{}{}",
        parameter_1, char_3);
}
void run() {
  char char_1{'w'};
  auto char_2 = char_1;
  char_1 = 'o';
  auto char_4 = char_1;
  char char_5{'f'};
  char_2 = 'o';
  char char_7{'b'};
  auto char_8 = char_2;
  char char_9{'l'};
  char_5 = '.';
  char char_11{'x'};
  auto &char_12 = char_11;
  auto char_13 = char_5;
  char char_14{'u'};
```

```
  function(char_5, char_12);
  auto char_15 = char_9;
  char char_16{'b'};
  auto char_17 = char_11;
  char_16 = 'i';
  auto char_19 = char_11;
  char char_20{'b'};
  auto char_21 = char_11;
  print("{}{}{}{}{}{}",
        char_17, char_13, char_20, char_1, char_8, char_15);
}

// Answer (8):

// __ __ __ __ __ __ __ __
```

**Puzzle 85**

```
auto function(char &parameter_1, char parameter_2) {
  parameter_1 = 'e';
  char char_2{'q'};
  auto char_3 = char_2;
  auto &char_4 = char_2;
  auto char_5 = char_4;
  print("{}{}{}",
        char_4, parameter_2, parameter_1);
}
void run() {
  char char_1{'e'};
  auto &char_2 = char_1;
  char char_3{'o'};
  auto char_4 = char_2;
  char_1 = 'y';
  auto &char_6 = char_2;
  auto char_7 = char_6;
  char char_8{'p'};
  auto char_9 = char_3;
  char_7 = 's';
  auto &char_11 = char_8;
  char_1 = 'u';
  function(char_3, char_2);
  char_6 = '.';
  auto char_14 = char_9;
```

```
  char char_15{'u'};
  char_3 = 'o';
  char char_17{'y'};
  auto char_18 = char_8;
  char char_19{'c'};
  auto char_20 = char_18;
  char_8 = 'n';
  auto char_22 = char_19;
  auto &char_23 = char_1;
  print("{}{}{}{}{}{}{}",
        char_15, char_4, char_6, char_19, char_14, char_11,
        char_7);
}

// Answer (10):

// __ __ __ __ __ __ __ __ __ __
```

**Puzzle 86**

```
auto function(char parameter_1, char &parameter_2) {
  parameter_1 = 'u';
  parameter_2 = 'l';
  char char_3{'p'};
  auto &char_4 = parameter_2;
  auto char_5 = char_4;
  auto &char_6 = char_4;
  print("{}{}{}",
        parameter_1, char_3, parameter_2);
}
void run() {
  char char_1{'u'};
  char_1 = 'l';
  auto &char_3 = char_1;
  char_1 = 't';
  print("{}",
        char_3);
  char char_5{'.'};
  function(char_3, char_1);
  auto char_6 = char_1;
  char_1 = 'p';
  auto char_8 = char_3;
  char_6 = 'm';
```

```
  auto char_10 = char_3;
  char char_11{'a'};
  auto &char_12 = char_10;
  char_8 = 'm';
  char char_14{'f'};
  auto &char_15 = char_11;
  auto char_16 = char_15;
  char_11 = 'y';
  char char_18{'l'};
  char_14 = 'x';
  auto char_20 = char_10;
  auto &char_21 = char_20;
  auto char_22 = char_14;
  auto &char_23 = char_8;
  char_14 = 'e';
  auto char_25 = char_18;
  print("{}{}{}{}{}{}{}",
        char_14, char_5, char_16, char_1, char_12, char_25,
        char_11);
}

// Answer (11):

// __ __ __ __ __ __ __ __ __ __ __
```

**Puzzle 87**

```
auto function(char parameter_1, char &parameter_2) {
  char char_1{'.'};
  auto &char_2 = parameter_1;
  print("{}{}",
        parameter_2, char_2);
  char_1 = 'n';
  auto &char_4 = char_1;
  auto char_5 = char_4;
  print("{}",
        char_4);
}
void run() {
  char char_1{'.'};
  char char_2{'a'};
  auto &char_3 = char_2;
  auto char_4 = char_3;
```

```
  char char_5{'g'};
  auto char_6 = char_1;
  char char_7{'r'};
  auto &char_8 = char_5;
  auto char_9 = char_8;
  char char_10{'r'};
  function(char_2, char_10);
  char_9 = 'e';
  print("{}{}{}{}",
        char_5, char_9, char_6, char_7);
  char char_12{'v'};
  auto char_13 = char_2;
  auto &char_14 = char_13;
  char_13 = 'e';
  char char_16{'i'};
  char_16 = 'e';
  char char_18{'h'};
  auto &char_19 = char_18;
  char char_20{'n'};
  auto char_21 = char_19;
  print("{}{}{}{}",
        char_4, char_20, char_8, char_13);
}

// Answer (11):

// __ __ __ __ __ __ __ __ __ __ __
```

**Puzzle 88**

```
auto function(char &parameter_1, char &parameter_2) {
  parameter_2 = 'l';
  char char_2{'c'};
  auto char_3 = char_2;
  char char_4{'s'};
  print("{}",
        char_3);
  auto &char_5 = char_4;
  print("{}",
        parameter_2);
}
void run() {
  char char_1{'l'};
```

```
  char_1 = 'c';
  auto char_3 = char_1;
  char_1 = 's';
  auto char_5 = char_1;
  char char_6{'t'};
  auto char_7 = char_6;
  char_3 = 'k';
  char char_9{'v'};
  function(char_5, char_7);
  auto &char_10 = char_5;
  char_1 = 'c';
  auto char_12 = char_5;
  char char_13{'j'};
  auto char_14 = char_13;
  char_6 = 'a';
  char char_16{'o'};
  auto char_17 = char_6;
  char_14 = '.';
  auto &char_19 = char_13;
  auto char_20 = char_14;
  auto &char_21 = char_10;
  char_19 = 'n';
  auto &char_23 = char_16;
  auto char_24 = char_20;
  auto &char_25 = char_7;
  print("{}{}{}{}{}{}{}{}",
        char_17, char_10, char_5, char_24, char_1, char_23,
        char_19, char_9);
}

// Answer (10):

// __ __ __ __ __ __ __ __ __ __
```

# std::swap

**Swap Example 1**

```
void run()
{
  int value = 4;
  int value2 = 2;
  print("{}{}", value, value2);
}

// Answer: 42
```

**Swap Example 2**

```
void run()
{
  int value = 4;
  int value2 = 2;
  std::swap(value, value2);
  print("{}{}", value, value2);
}

// Answer: 24
```

# char std::swap Puzzles

**Puzzle 89**

```
void run() {
  char char_1{'r'};
  auto &char_2 = char_1;
  char_2 = 'w';
  print("{}",
        char_2);
  char_1 = 'c';
  auto char_5 = char_2;
  char_2 = 'm';
  char char_7{'i'};
  auto char_8 = char_1;
  auto &char_9 = char_1;
  char char_10{'n'};
  auto char_11 = char_5;
  char char_12{'o'};
  char_12 = 'j';
  std::swap(char_1, char_2);
  auto &char_14 = char_1;
  print("{}{}{}",
        char_11, char_7, char_10);
}

// Answer (4):

// __ __ __ __
```

**Puzzle 90**

```
void run() {
  char char_1{'S'};
  auto char_2 = char_1;
  char_2 = 'x';
  auto char_4 = char_1;
  char char_5{'s'};
  auto &char_6 = char_1;
  char char_7{'y'};
  auto &char_8 = char_4;
```

```
  char_1 = 'h';
  auto char_10 = char_5;
  char_5 = 'F';
  char char_12{'v'};
  char_1 = 'k';
  auto &char_14 = char_4;
  char char_15{'L'};
  print("{}{}{}",
        char_15, char_5, char_14);
}

// Answer (3):

// __ __ __
```

**Puzzle 91**

```
void run() {
  char char_1{'l'};
  print("{}",
        char_1);
  auto char_2 = char_1;
  auto &char_3 = char_1;
  char char_4{'r'};
  char_3 = 's';
  print("{}{}",
        char_2, char_4);
  auto char_6 = char_3;
  auto &char_7 = char_1;
  char char_8{'f'};
  auto &char_9 = char_4;
  char_6 = 't';
  char char_11{'i'};
  char_3 = 'n';
  auto char_13 = char_11;
  char char_14{'m'};
  auto &char_15 = char_4;
  char char_16{'s'};
  print("{}{}{}{}",
        char_11, char_3, char_6, char_8);
}

// Answer (7):
```

```
// __ __ __ __ __ __ __
```

**Puzzle 92**

```
void run() {
  char char_1{'p'};
  char_1 = 'c';
  auto &char_3 = char_1;
  std::swap(char_1, char_3);
  char char_4{'d'};
  auto &char_5 = char_1;
  auto char_6 = char_1;
  auto &char_7 = char_1;
  auto char_8 = char_7;
  auto &char_9 = char_3;
  char_8 = 'f';
  char char_11{'e'};
  char_9 = 'i';
  auto char_13 = char_4;
  auto &char_14 = char_3;
  std::swap(char_8, char_1);
  auto char_15 = char_1;
  char char_16{'m'};
  auto char_17 = char_7;
  print("{}{}{}{}{}",
        char_7, char_13, char_8, char_16, char_3);
}

// Answer (5):

// __ __ __ __ __
```

**Puzzle 93**

```
void run() {
  char char_1{'c'};
  char_1 = 'l';
  auto char_3 = char_1;
  auto &char_4 = char_1;
  char_4 = 'r';
  auto &char_6 = char_3;
  auto char_7 = char_1;
  char_7 = 'p';
  char char_9{'v'};
  char_9 = 'o';
  char char_11{'e'};
  std::swap(char_4, char_1);
  auto &char_12 = char_6;
  auto char_13 = char_11;
  auto &char_14 = char_9;
  std::swap(char_13, char_11);
  auto char_15 = char_7;
  print("{}{}{}",
        char_1, char_11, char_12);
  char char_16{'k'};
  auto &char_17 = char_13;
  char_13 = 's';
  auto &char_19 = char_11;
  char char_20{'_'};
  std::swap(char_11, char_1);
  char char_21{'v'};
  print("{}{}{}{}",
        char_20, char_9, char_7, char_17);
}

// Answer (7):

// __ __ __ __ __ __ __
```

**Puzzle 94**

```
void run() {
  char char_1{'t'};
  char_1 = 'p';
  char char_3{'o'};
  char_3 = 'y';
  std::swap(char_1, char_3);
  char_1 = 'w';
  char char_6{'s'};
  print("{}{}",
        char_6, char_1);
  char_3 = 'o';
  char char_8{'w'};
  auto char_9 = char_8;
  char char_10{'a'};
  std::swap(char_10, char_9);
  char char_11{'b'};
  char_11 = 'd';
  auto &char_13 = char_6;
  char_9 = 'j';
  char char_15{'w'};
  std::swap(char_9, char_15);
  char_15 = 't';
  char char_17{'f'};
  auto char_18 = char_1;
  char_18 = 'a';
  char char_20{'c'};
  auto &char_21 = char_18;
  char char_22{'n'};
  auto char_23 = char_9;
  auto &char_24 = char_22;
  auto char_25 = char_10;
  print("{}{}{}{}{}",
        char_13, char_20, char_18, char_24, char_17);
}

// Answer (7):

// __ __ __ __ __ __ __
```

**Puzzle 95**

```
void run() {
  char char_1{'f'};
  auto char_2 = char_1;
  char_2 = 'q';
  std::swap(char_2, char_1);
  print("{}",
        char_2);
  char_1 = 't';
  auto &char_5 = char_1;
  std::swap(char_2, char_1);
  char char_6{'u'};
  auto char_7 = char_5;
  char char_8{'f'};
  auto &char_9 = char_6;
  char_8 = 'c';
  std::swap(char_2, char_5);
  char_9 = 'e';
  print("{}{}{}",
        char_6, char_5, char_9);
  std::swap(char_6, char_8);
  char_2 = 'e';
  auto char_13 = char_2;
  char_7 = 'v';
  auto &char_15 = char_5;
  char_8 = 'g';
  auto &char_17 = char_7;
  std::swap(char_9, char_7);
  auto char_18 = char_5;
  auto &char_19 = char_18;
  char_6 = 'l';
  char char_21{'s'};
  auto &char_22 = char_5;
  print("{}{}{}",
        char_21, char_1, char_13);
  char char_23{'p'};
  char_22 = 'k';
  char char_25{'x'};
  char_22 = 'a';
  auto char_27 = char_23;
  char char_28{'t'};
  char_15 = 'e';
```

```
  auto char_30 = char_15;
  print("{}{}{}{}{}",
        char_25, char_17, char_15, char_23, char_28);
}

// Answer (12):

// __ __ __ __ __ __ __ __ __ __ __ __
```

**Puzzle 96**

```
void run() {
  char char_1{'c'};
  auto char_2 = char_1;
  char char_3{'y'};
  auto char_4 = char_3;
  char char_5{'o'};
  char_4 = 'l';
  print("{}{}",
        char_1, char_5);
  char_1 = 'v';
  auto &char_8 = char_2;
  char_3 = 'n';
  char char_10{'q'};
  char_4 = 'd';
  auto char_12 = char_5;
  auto &char_13 = char_4;
  auto char_14 = char_1;
  char char_15{'x'};
  char_10 = 'd';
  auto char_17 = char_4;
  char char_18{'c'};
  std::swap(char_10, char_3);
  char_12 = 'c';
  auto &char_20 = char_14;
  char_18 = 'm';
  char char_22{'p'};
  char_4 = 'r';
  char char_24{'h'};
  auto &char_25 = char_5;
  char char_26{'w'};
  char_3 = '.';
  auto &char_28 = char_25;
```

```
  char_15 = 'l';
  auto char_30 = char_22;
  print("{}{}{}{}{}{}{}",
        char_10, char_14, char_3, char_22, char_4, char_28,
        char_18);
}

// Answer (9):

// __ __ __ __ __ __ __ __ __
```

**Puzzle 97**

```
auto function(char &parameter_1, char &parameter_2) {
  parameter_2 = 'g';
  print("{}",
        parameter_2);
  parameter_2 = 'r';
  print("{}",
        parameter_1);
  parameter_1 = 'r';
}
void run() {
  char char_1{'g'};
  auto &char_2 = char_1;
  char char_3{'r'};
  auto char_4 = char_3;
  char_1 = 'x';
  auto &char_6 = char_3;
  char char_7{'t'};
  auto &char_8 = char_3;
  std::swap(char_8, char_2);
  char_8 = 'r';
  function(char_2, char_7);
  char_1 = 'e';
  char char_11{'t'};
  char_7 = 'a';
  auto char_13 = char_1;
  char char_14{'o'};
  print("{}{}{}{}{}",
        char_2, char_7, char_11, char_1, char_8);
}
```

```
// Answer (7):

// __ __ __ __ __ __ __
```

**Puzzle 98**

```
auto function(char parameter_1, char &parameter_2) {
  char char_1{'S'};
  auto char_2 = parameter_1;
  char char_3{'N'};
  auto &char_4 = parameter_2;
  parameter_1 = 'F';
  auto &char_6 = char_1;
  print("{}{}",
        parameter_1, char_3);
}
void run() {
  char char_1{'S'};
  char char_2{'T'};
  auto &char_3 = char_2;
  auto char_4 = char_3;
  char char_5{'F'};
  auto &char_6 = char_2;
  char_3 = 'W';
  auto char_8 = char_5;
  function(char_1, char_4);
  auto char_9 = char_5;
  char_5 = 'f';
  auto &char_11 = char_1;
  char_8 = 'w';
  auto char_13 = char_3;
  char char_14{'t'};
  print("{}{}{}{}",
        char_11, char_4, char_1, char_13);
}

// Answer (6):

// __ __ __ __ __ __
```

**Puzzle 99**

```
auto function(char parameter_1, char &parameter_2) {
  char char_1{'s'};
  char char_2{'m'};
  auto &char_3 = char_2;
  char char_4{'e'};
  parameter_2 = 'q';
  auto char_6 = char_3;
  print("{}{}{}",
        char_6, char_4, char_3);
}
void run() {
  char char_1{'s'};
  auto char_2 = char_1;
  char char_3{'f'};
  char_2 = 'e';
  auto char_5 = char_2;
  function(char_5, char_3);
  char_5 = 'c';
  auto &char_7 = char_1;
  char_5 = 'r';
  auto char_9 = char_2;
  auto &char_10 = char_7;
  auto char_11 = char_9;
  char_3 = 'a';
  auto char_13 = char_7;
  auto &char_14 = char_9;
  auto char_15 = char_3;
  char char_16{'.'};
  auto &char_17 = char_5;
  print("{}{}{}{}",
        char_16, char_5, char_11, char_7);
}

// Answer (7):

// __ __ __ __ __ __ __
```

**Puzzle 100**

```
auto function(char &parameter_1, char parameter_2) {
  std::swap(parameter_2, parameter_1);
  parameter_1 = 'u';
  std::swap(parameter_1, parameter_2);
  char char_2{'t'};
  char_2 = 't';
  auto &char_4 = parameter_1;
  print("{}{}",
        char_2, parameter_2);
}
void run() {
  char char_1{'u'};
  auto char_2 = char_1;
  std::swap(char_2, char_1);
  char char_3{'t'};
  char_1 = 'e';
  auto &char_5 = char_3;
  char char_6{'p'};
  std::swap(char_2, char_1);
  print("{}{}{}",
        char_3, char_1, char_6);
  auto char_7 = char_1;
  char_1 = 'l';
  std::swap(char_1, char_7);
  char char_9{'e'};
  char_6 = 'p';
  auto &char_11 = char_2;
  char char_12{'l'};
  auto char_13 = char_6;
  char_6 = 'y';
  char char_15{'m'};
  auto &char_16 = char_7;
  char char_17{'.'};
  auto &char_18 = char_12;
  print("{}{}{}",
        char_18, char_11, char_17);
  function(char_7, char_2);
  print("{}{}{}",
        char_13, char_16, char_9);
}
```

```
// Answer (11):

// __ __ __ __ __ __ __ __ __ __ __
```

**Puzzle 101**

```
auto function(char &parameter_1, char &parameter_2) {
  parameter_2 = 'c';
  std::swap(parameter_1, parameter_2);
  char char_2{'w'};
  auto &char_3 = parameter_1;
  parameter_2 = 'q';
  char char_5{'d'};
  print("{}{}",
        char_5, char_3);
}
void run() {
  char char_1{'c'};
  char_1 = 'a';
  auto &char_3 = char_1;
  auto char_4 = char_1;
  auto &char_5 = char_3;
  auto char_6 = char_4;
  std::swap(char_3, char_4);
  function(char_6, char_5);
  char char_7{'e'};
  auto char_8 = char_6;
  char_4 = 't';
  char char_10{'w'};
  char_5 = 'd';
  std::swap(char_4, char_3);
  char char_12{'f'};
  auto char_13 = char_10;
  char char_14{'j'};
  auto char_15 = char_3;
  char_8 = 'k';
  char char_17{'f'};
  auto char_18 = char_12;
  char_13 = '.';
  char char_20{'l'};
  char_10 = '.';
  auto &char_22 = char_7;
  print("{}{}{}{}{}{}{}{}{}",
```

```
        char_20, char_13, char_18, char_6, char_3, char_10,
        char_4, char_7, char_17);
}

// Answer (11):

// __ __ __ __ __ __ __ __ __ __ __
```

**Puzzle 102**

```
auto function(char &parameter_1, char parameter_2) {
  std::swap(parameter_1, parameter_2);
  char char_1{'l'};
  std::swap(parameter_2, parameter_1);
  parameter_2 = 'j';
  auto char_3 = char_1;
  char_3 = 'o';
  print("{}",
        char_3);
}
void run() {
  char char_1{'h'};
  char_1 = 'r';
  auto char_3 = char_1;
  char_3 = 'o';
  std::swap(char_3, char_1);
  char_1 = 't';
  std::swap(char_1, char_3);
  auto char_6 = char_3;
  char_6 = 'e';
  print("{}",
        char_3);
  auto char_8 = char_1;
  char_8 = 'b';
  auto &char_10 = char_8;
  function(char_6, char_3);
  auto &char_11 = char_3;
  char char_12{'r'};
  std::swap(char_3, char_1);
  char_1 = 'o';
  auto &char_14 = char_12;
  char char_15{'b'};
  char_10 = 'p';
```

```
  auto char_17 = char_15;
  char_10 = 'l';
  char char_19{'q'};
  char_15 = 'r';
  char char_21{'j'};
  char_3 = 'q';
  auto char_23 = char_3;
  auto &char_24 = char_14;
  char_12 = 'w';
  auto &char_26 = char_12;
  char char_27{'o'};
  auto char_28 = char_6;
  print("{}{}{}{}{}{}",
        char_14, char_8, char_1, char_24, char_6, char_15);
}

// Answer (8):

// __ __ __ __ __ __ __ __
```

**Puzzle 103**

```
auto function(char parameter_1, char &parameter_2) {
  parameter_2 = 'r';
  char char_2{'c'};
  auto char_3 = parameter_1;
  print("{}",
        char_2);
  parameter_1 = 'h';
  auto char_5 = char_3;
  print("{}",
        char_3);
}
void run() {
  char char_1{'u'};
  auto &char_2 = char_1;
  auto char_3 = char_2;
  char_2 = 's';
  auto char_5 = char_1;
  char_1 = 'r';
  auto &char_7 = char_3;
  std::swap(char_2, char_5);
  auto &char_8 = char_2;
```

```
  char char_9{'p'};
  auto &char_10 = char_5;
  char char_11{'s'};
  auto &char_12 = char_5;
  char_1 = 'k';
  char char_14{'e'};
  function(char_9, char_8);
  char_8 = '.';
  char char_16{'y'};
  char_7 = 'n';
  auto char_18 = char_7;
  char char_19{'j'};
  auto char_20 = char_10;
  char char_21{'r'};
  auto &char_22 = char_7;
  auto char_23 = char_9;
  char char_24{'o'};
  print("{}{}{}{}{}{}{}",
        char_23, char_2, char_14, char_12, char_20, char_24,
        char_21);
}

// Answer (9):

// __ __ __ __ __ __ __ __ __
```

**Puzzle 104**

```
auto function(char parameter_1, char &parameter_2) {
  char char_1{'n'};
  auto &char_2 = parameter_1;
  parameter_1 = 'c';
  auto &char_4 = char_2;
  parameter_1 = 'u';
  print("{}{}",
        char_4, char_1);
}
void run() {
  char char_1{'n'};
  char char_2{'d'};
  char_1 = 'c';
  auto char_4 = char_1;
  auto &char_5 = char_4;
```

```
  auto char_6 = char_4;
  auto &char_7 = char_4;
  char char_8{'m'};
  function(char_2, char_1);
  auto &char_9 = char_8;
  char char_10{'e'};
  auto &char_11 = char_9;
  auto char_12 = char_2;
  char char_13{'t'};
  char_2 = 'x';
  auto &char_15 = char_10;
  char char_16{'e'};
  auto char_17 = char_16;
  auto &char_18 = char_16;
  char char_19{'p'};
  std::swap(char_9, char_4);
  auto &char_20 = char_2;
  auto char_21 = char_1;
  auto &char_22 = char_12;
  print("{}{}{}{}{}{}{}{}",
        char_16, char_2, char_19, char_15, char_6, char_13,
        char_17, char_12);
}

// Answer (10):

// __ __ __ __ __ __ __ __ __ __
```

# std::exchange

**Exchange Example 1**

```
void run()
{
  int value = 4;
  int value2 = 2;
  print("{}{}", value, value2);
}

// Answer: 42
```

**Exchange Example 2**

```
void run()
{
  int value = 4;
  int value2 = 2;

  value2 = std::exchange(value, 3);
  print("{}{}", value, value2);
}

// Answer: 34
```

# char std::exchange Puzzles

**Puzzle 105**

```
void run() {
  char char_1{'d'};
  auto &char_2 = char_1;
  auto char_3 = char_1;
  char_1 = 'P';
  auto char_5 = char_2;
  char_3 = 'M';
  char char_7{'j'};
  auto char_8 = char_2;
  char char_9{'O'};
  char_2 = std::exchange(char_5, char{'C'});
  char char_11{'F'};
  auto char_12 = char_5;
  char char_13{'s'};
  print("{}{}{}{}{}{}",
        char_11, char_5, char_9, char_3, char_1, char_2);
}

// Answer (6):

// __ __ __ __ __ __
```

**Puzzle 106**

```
void run() {
  char char_1{'y'};
  auto char_2 = char_1;
  char char_3{'D'};
  char_2 = 'F';
  auto char_5 = char_3;
  char char_6{'r'};
  char_6 = 'A';
  auto &char_8 = char_5;
  auto char_9 = char_3;
  auto &char_10 = char_6;
  char char_11{'b'};
  auto &char_12 = char_11;
```

```
  auto char_13 = char_3;
  print("{}{}{}{}",
        char_2, char_6, char_13, char_3);
}

// Answer (4):

// __ __ __ __
```

**Puzzle 107**

```
void run() {
  char char_1{'l'};
  char char_2{'c'};
  char_1 = 'r';
  print("{}",
        char_2);
  auto &char_4 = char_2;
  char char_5{'h'};
  auto char_6 = char_4;
  char_2 = std::exchange(char_1, char{'e'});
  char char_8{'p'};
  char_4 = std::exchange(char_2, char{'c'});
  auto char_10 = char_2;
  char char_11{'o'};
  char_4 = 'e';
  char char_13{'a'};
  auto char_14 = char_13;
  char char_15{'s'};
  auto &char_16 = char_13;
  char_14 = 'm';
  char char_18{'v'};
  print("{}{}{}{}{}{}",
        char_11, char_14, char_8, char_16, char_10, char_1);
}

// Answer (7):

// __ __ __ __ __ __ __
```

**Puzzle 108**

```
void run() {
  char char_1{'m'};
  char char_2{'l'};
  char_1 = 'o';
  char char_4{'a'};
  char_2 = std::exchange(char_1, char{'a'});
  auto &char_6 = char_2;
  char_4 = 'P';
  char char_8{'O'};
  auto &char_9 = char_6;
  char_2 = 'y';
  auto &char_11 = char_4;
  char char_12{'A'};
  char_1 = std::exchange(char_6, char{'q'});
  auto char_14 = char_11;
  char_6 = std::exchange(char_2, char{'d'});
  auto char_16 = char_2;
  char_16 = 'v';
  auto char_18 = char_6;
  auto &char_19 = char_11;
  char char_20{'e'};
  auto &char_21 = char_14;
  print("{}{}{}{}",
        char_19, char_8, char_4, char_12);
}

// Answer (4):

// __ __ __ __
```

**Puzzle 109**

```
void run() {
  char char_1{'i'};
  auto char_2 = char_1;
  char char_3{'e'};
  auto char_4 = char_2;
  char_1 = std::exchange(char_2, char{'.'});
  char char_6{'l'};
  auto char_7 = char_6;
  char char_8{'s'};
```

```
  char_6 = 'x';
  char_3 = std::exchange(char_2, char{'n'});
  auto char_11 = char_7;
  char_6 = 'i';
  char char_13{'s'};
  char_7 = 't';
  auto &char_15 = char_11;
  char_11 = 'v';
  char char_17{'e'};
  char_13 = 's';
  print("{}{}{}{}{}",
        char_4, char_2, char_7, char_13, char_17);
  char_15 = 'u';
  char char_20{'q'};
  char_20 = std::exchange(char_7, char{'w'});
  char char_22{'q'};
  char_17 = std::exchange(char_1, char{'q'});
  char_11 = 'e';
  auto &char_25 = char_2;
  char char_26{'o'};
  print("{}{}{}{}",
        char_22, char_3, char_6, char_25);
  auto char_27 = char_1;
  print("{}{}{}{}",
        char_20, char_8, char_15, char_27);
}

// Answer (13):

// __ __ __ __ __ __ __ __ __ __ __ __ __
```

**Puzzle 110**

```
void run() {
  char char_1{'c'};
  auto &char_2 = char_1;
  char_1 = std::exchange(char_2, char{'i'});
  char char_4{'h'};
  print("{}",
        char_1);
  char char_5{'r'};
  auto char_6 = char_4;
  char_6 = std::exchange(char_4, char{'o'});
```

```
  char char_8{'l'};
  auto char_9 = char_5;
  print("{}{}{}",
        char_6, char_9, char_4);
  char_1 = ':';
  auto char_11 = char_8;
  char char_12{'n'};
  char_11 = 'y';
  auto &char_14 = char_5;
  char char_15{'b'};
  char_4 = 'i';
  auto &char_17 = char_1;
  char_14 = 'o';
  char char_19{'a'};
  print("{}{}{}{}",
        char_12, char_14, char_2, char_17);
  char_14 = 'j';
  auto char_21 = char_4;
  char char_22{'s'};
  auto &char_23 = char_12;
  char char_24{'m'};
  print("{}{}{}",
        char_19, char_15, char_22);
}

// Answer (11):

// __ __ __ __ __ __ __ __ __ __ __
```

**Puzzle 111**

```
void run() {
  char char_1{'h'};
  char_1 = 'j';
  char char_3{'m'};
  char_1 = 'e';
  char char_5{'t'};
  auto char_6 = char_5;
  char char_7{'h'};
  auto &char_8 = char_1;
  char char_9{'i'};
  char_3 = 's';
  char char_11{'a'};
```

```
  auto char_12 = char_11;
  char_1 = 'k';
  auto char_14 = char_6;
  auto &char_15 = char_3;
  char char_16{'c'};
  char_1 = 'p';
  auto char_18 = char_1;
  char_14 = 'g';
  char_14 = std::exchange(char_1, char{'j'});
  auto &char_21 = char_6;
  char char_22{'n'};
  char_14 = std::exchange(char_18, char{'s'});
  print("{}{}{}{}{}{}",
        char_18, char_5, char_12, char_21, char_9, char_16);
  char char_24{'x'};
  auto char_25 = char_8;
  char_24 = '_';
  char_8 = std::exchange(char_6, char{'f'});
  char char_28{'c'};
  char_22 = 't';
  char char_30{'c'};
  print("{}{}{}{}{}",
        char_24, char_30, char_11, char_3, char_22);
}

// Answer (11):

// __ __ __ __ __ __ __ __ __ __ __
```

**Puzzle 112**

```
void run() {
  char char_1{'b'};
  auto &char_2 = char_1;
  char_2 = 'e';
  char char_4{'s'};
  auto &char_5 = char_4;
  print("{}",
        char_5);
  char char_6{'h'};
  auto &char_7 = char_5;
  auto char_8 = char_2;
  auto &char_9 = char_4;
```

```
  char_4 = 'g';
  char char_11{'n'};
  auto &char_12 = char_8;
  char char_13{'q'};
  char_6 = 'd';
  char char_15{'g'};
  auto &char_16 = char_12;
  char char_17{'p'};
  auto char_18 = char_1;
  char_16 = 'y';
  char char_20{'j'};
  auto &char_21 = char_7;
  char char_22{'w'};
  char_12 = std::exchange(char_9, char{'w'});
  char_4 = 't';
  auto &char_25 = char_4;
  char_20 = 'x';
  char char_27{'u'};
  print("{}{}{}{}{}{}",
        char_25, char_27, char_6, char_18, char_11, char_7);
}

// Answer (7):

// __ __ __ __ __ __ __
```

**Puzzle 113**

```
auto function(char &parameter_1, char parameter_2) {
  char char_1{'i'};
  char_1 = 'r';
  char char_3{'s'};
  parameter_1 = 'b';
  char char_5{'s'};
  parameter_1 = 'o';
  print("{}{}",
        char_3, parameter_2);
}
void run() {
  char char_1{'i'};
  auto &char_2 = char_1;
  auto char_3 = char_1;
  char char_4{'y'};
```

```
  char_2 = std::exchange(char_3, char{'s'});
  char char_6{'o'};
  print("{}{}",
        char_1, char_6);
  char_1 = 'g';
  char char_8{'s'};
  char_4 = 'a';
  auto &char_10 = char_8;
  char char_11{'b'};
  std::swap(char_6, char_4);
  char char_12{'a'};
  auto &char_13 = char_1;
  char char_14{'_'};
  char_4 = std::exchange(char_3, char{'j'});
  char char_16{'f'};
  char_10 = std::exchange(char_4, char{'n'});
  function(char_2, char_14);
  auto &char_18 = char_8;
  char char_19{'e'};
  auto &char_20 = char_11;
  print("{}{}{}{}",
        char_11, char_12, char_10, char_19);
}

// Answer (8):

// __ __ __ __ __ __ __ __
```

**Puzzle 114**

```
auto function(char &parameter_1, char &parameter_2) {
  parameter_1 = 'k';
  parameter_2 = 'c';
  char char_3{'o'};
  parameter_1 = 'j';
  print("{}{}",
        parameter_2, char_3);
  char char_5{'n'};
  print("{}",
        char_5);
}
void run() {
  char char_1{'d'};
```

```
    auto &char_2 = char_1;
    char char_3{'o'};
    auto char_4 = char_1;
    char_3 = 'n';
    auto &char_6 = char_3;
    char char_7{'p'};
    char_4 = 'k';
    auto char_9 = char_1;
    char char_10{'k'};
    auto char_11 = char_4;
    char_10 = std::exchange(char_9, char{'q'});
    char_2 = 'n';
    auto &char_14 = char_9;
    char_2 = 'j';
    auto char_16 = char_3;
    auto &char_17 = char_14;
    std::swap(char_16, char_6);
    function(char_17, char_1);
    char_17 = std::exchange(char_2, char{'v'});
    auto char_19 = char_17;
    char char_20{'a'};
    char_6 = 'r';
    char char_22{'.'};
    char_9 = 'e';
    auto &char_24 = char_2;
    print("{}{}{}{}{}{}",
          char_1, char_22, char_3, char_20, char_16, char_4);
}

// Answer (9):

// __ __ __ __ __ __ __ __ __
```

**Puzzle 115**

```
auto function(char parameter_1, char &parameter_2) {
  parameter_1 = 'e';
  parameter_2 = std::exchange(parameter_1, char{'y'});
  char char_3{'m'};
  char_3 = 'n';
  auto &char_5 = char_3;
  auto char_6 = char_3;
  print("{}{}",
        parameter_2, char_6);
}
void run() {
  char char_1{'e'};
  auto char_2 = char_1;
  char char_3{'q'};
  auto char_4 = char_2;
  char_3 = 'l';
  char char_6{'c'};
  char_4 = 'a';
  char char_8{'g'};
  print("{}{}{}",
        char_3, char_1, char_8);
  auto char_9 = char_2;
  char char_10{'l'};
  function(char_4, char_3);
  auto char_11 = char_9;
  char char_12{'j'};
  char_1 = 'c';
  std::swap(char_6, char_9);
  auto char_14 = char_6;
  char_9 = 'y';
  char char_16{'x'};
  auto &char_17 = char_11;
  char_1 = 'd';
  char_4 = std::exchange(char_3, char{'h'});
  char char_20{'d'};
  char_1 = 'u';
  char_11 = std::exchange(char_8, char{'f'});
  auto &char_23 = char_8;
  char char_24{'r'};
  print("{}{}{}{}",
        char_20, char_24, char_6, char_10);
```

```
}

// Answer (9):

// __ __ __ __ __ __ __ __ __
```

**Puzzle 116**

```
auto function(char &parameter_1, char &parameter_2) {
  char char_1{'e'};
  auto &char_2 = parameter_2;
  auto char_3 = char_2;
  char char_4{'d'};
  char_3 = 'u';
  parameter_1 = std::exchange(char_1, char{'r'});
  print("{}{}",
        parameter_2, char_3);
}
void run() {
  char char_1{'e'};
  auto char_2 = char_1;
  char char_3{'q'};
  char_1 = 'd';
  char char_5{'u'};
  char_5 = 'v';
  char char_7{'c'};
  auto char_8 = char_5;
  auto &char_9 = char_2;
  auto char_10 = char_9;
  std::swap(char_5, char_9);
  function(char_10, char_3);
  char_8 = std::exchange(char_10, char{'n'});
  auto char_12 = char_9;
  char_2 = std::exchange(char_3, char{'e'});
  auto char_14 = char_3;
  char_12 = 'a';
  char_2 = std::exchange(char_14, char{'j'});
  auto &char_17 = char_7;
  char char_18{'l'};
  auto char_19 = char_5;
  char_3 = std::exchange(char_19, char{'k'});
  char_19 = 'u';
  char_8 = std::exchange(char_7, char{'.'});
```

```
  function(char_12, char_3);
  char_19 = std::exchange(char_12, char{'s'});
  auto &char_24 = char_10;
  char_12 = 'u';
  auto &char_26 = char_14;
  auto char_27 = char_9;
  char_8 = 'x';
  char_26 = std::exchange(char_24, char{'f'});
  auto &char_30 = char_3;
  print("{}{}{}{}{}{}",
        char_30, char_7, char_1, char_2, char_24, char_26);
}

// Answer (10):

// __ __ __ __ __ __ __ __ __ __
```

**Puzzle 117**

```
auto function(char &parameter_1, char parameter_2) {
  char char_1{'m'};
  char char_2{'o'};
  auto &char_3 = char_1;
  std::swap(parameter_2, char_1);
  char char_4{'g'};
  print("{}{}",
        parameter_2, char_1);
}
void run() {
  char char_1{'m'};
  auto &char_2 = char_1;
  char char_3{'h'};
  std::swap(char_3, char_2);
  auto char_4 = char_1;
  std::swap(char_2, char_4);
  char char_5{'e'};
  function(char_3, char_5);
  char_4 = 'f';
  char_3 = std::exchange(char_2, char{'i'});
  char_1 = '_';
  char char_9{'u'};
  auto &char_10 = char_4;
  char char_11{'n'};
```

```
  char_3 = 'r';
  char char_13{'1'};
  auto &char_14 = char_1;
  function(char_13, char_1);
  char_1 = 'n';
  char_4 = std::exchange(char_9, char{'_'});
  auto char_17 = char_9;
  char char_18{'p'};
  auto &char_19 = char_18;
  char char_20{'d'};
  std::swap(char_2, char_1);
  auto &char_21 = char_4;
  char_11 = 'f';
  auto &char_23 = char_18;
  auto char_24 = char_9;
  char_9 = 'n';
  char_19 = std::exchange(char_2, char{'t'});
  char char_27{'f'};
  print("{}{}{}{}{}{}",
        char_27, char_10, char_9, char_13, char_24, char_14);
}

// Answer (10):

// __ __ __ __ __ __ __ __ __ __
```

**Puzzle 118**

```
auto function(char &parameter_1, char parameter_2) {
  parameter_1 = std::exchange(parameter_2, char{'u'});
  parameter_2 = 't';
  parameter_1 = std::exchange(parameter_2, char{'n'});
  char char_4{'p'};
  auto &char_5 = parameter_1;
  char char_6{'w'};
  print("{}{}",
        char_4, char_5);
}
void run() {
  char char_1{'o'};
  char char_2{'t'};
  char_1 = 'o';
  auto char_4 = char_1;
```

```
  auto &char_5 = char_4;
  std::swap(char_1, char_2);
  char char_6{'x'};
  char_4 = 'p';
  auto char_8 = char_5;
  std::swap(char_5, char_4);
  auto char_9 = char_6;
  auto &char_10 = char_6;
  char char_11{'c'};
  std::swap(char_1, char_10);
  auto char_12 = char_5;
  auto &char_13 = char_8;
  char_11 = 'd';
  auto char_15 = char_6;
  auto &char_16 = char_8;
  char_5 = std::exchange(char_8, char{'i'});
  char_5 = 'f';
  function(char_16, char_1);
  char_12 = 'e';
  char char_20{'i'};
  auto char_21 = char_10;
  char_6 = std::exchange(char_5, char{'_'});
  auto &char_23 = char_4;
  char_2 = 't';
  std::swap(char_13, char_6);
  char_9 = std::exchange(char_20, char{'d'});
  auto &char_26 = char_20;
  char_1 = 'r';
  char char_28{'i'};
  print("{}{}{}{}{}{}{}",
        char_1, char_11, char_9, char_13, char_16, char_23,
        char_6);
}

// Answer (9):

// __ __ __ __ __ __ __ __ __
```

**Puzzle 119**

```
auto function(char parameter_1, char &parameter_2) {
  print("{}",
        parameter_2);
  parameter_1 = std::exchange(parameter_2, char{'u'});
  parameter_2 = 't';
  parameter_2 = std::exchange(parameter_1, char{'e'});
  print("{}",
        parameter_1);
  parameter_2 = 't';
}
void run() {
  char char_1{'n'};
  char_1 = 't';
  auto char_3 = char_1;
  auto &char_4 = char_1;
  char_4 = std::exchange(char_3, char{'e'});
  char char_6{'r'};
  std::swap(char_6, char_3);
  auto char_7 = char_4;
  char char_8{'e'};
  char_8 = 'k';
  auto &char_10 = char_1;
  char char_11{'b'};
  auto &char_12 = char_10;
  std::swap(char_3, char_11);
  auto char_13 = char_8;
  char_13 = 'i';
  auto char_15 = char_6;
  std::swap(char_7, char_13);
  function(char_12, char_11);
  auto char_16 = char_10;
  auto &char_17 = char_7;
  char_13 = '.';
  char char_19{'o'};
  char_12 = 'd';
  char_12 = std::exchange(char_17, char{'o'});
  auto &char_22 = char_16;
  char_3 = 'o';
  char char_24{'r'};
  auto char_25 = char_13;
  auto &char_26 = char_17;
```

```
  auto char_27 = char_1;
  print("{}{}{}{}{}{}{}{}",
        char_13, char_22, char_26, char_8, char_27, char_11,
        char_6, char_24);
}

// Answer (10):

// __ __ __ __ __ __ __ __ __ __
```

**Puzzle 120**

```
auto function(char &parameter_1, char parameter_2) {
  parameter_2 = 'm';
  std::swap(parameter_2, parameter_1);
  char char_2{'q'};
  char_2 = 'm';
  auto &char_4 = char_2;
  auto char_5 = parameter_2;
  print("{}",
        parameter_2);
}
void run() {
  char char_1{'m'};
  auto char_2 = char_1;
  auto &char_3 = char_1;
  char char_4{'f'};
  auto char_5 = char_1;
  char char_6{'f'};
  auto char_7 = char_6;
  char char_8{'g'};
  function(char_6, char_1);
  std::swap(char_2, char_1);
  auto &char_9 = char_8;
  char_7 = 'k';
  char char_11{'u'};
  function(char_11, char_5);
  char char_12{'l'};
  auto char_13 = char_3;
  char_2 = 'p';
  auto &char_15 = char_1;
  char char_16{'.'};
  std::swap(char_3, char_9);
```

```
  char_11 = 'n';
  char_12 = std::exchange(char_4, char{'p'});
  auto char_19 = char_13;
  char_3 = 'e';
  auto char_21 = char_4;
  char_6 = 'y';
  char char_23{'n'};
  auto &char_24 = char_5;
  char char_25{'l'};
  char_5 = std::exchange(char_3, char{'c'});
  auto char_27 = char_5;
  print("{}{}{}{}{}{}{}{}",
        char_11, char_1, char_16, char_9, char_24, char_13,
        char_12, char_23);
}

// Answer (10):

// __ __ __ __ __ __ __ __ __ __
```

**Puzzle 121**

```
auto function(char &parameter_1, char parameter_2) {
  parameter_2 = 's';
  char char_2{'i'};
  print("{}",
        parameter_2);
  char char_3{'c'};
  char_3 = std::exchange(char_2, char{'e'});
  auto &char_5 = char_3;
  print("{}",
        char_2);
}
void run() {
  char char_1{'s'};
  char_1 = 'w';
  char char_3{'x'};
  char_3 = 'e';
  auto &char_5 = char_3;
  char char_6{'u'};
  auto char_7 = char_3;
  char char_8{'y'};
  std::swap(char_6, char_5);
```

```
  auto &char_9 = char_3;
  char_6 = 'd';
  char char_11{'r'};
  char_3 = 'q';
  auto &char_13 = char_7;
  std::swap(char_9, char_1);
  char char_14{'s'};
  char_5 = 'e';
  char char_16{'i'};
  char_11 = 'n';
  std::swap(char_11, char_9);
  auto char_18 = char_16;
  char_7 = 'o';
  char char_20{'f'};
  auto &char_21 = char_14;
  char char_22{'_'};
  auto &char_23 = char_20;
  char_8 = 'b';
  char char_25{'a'};
  auto char_26 = char_22;
  function(char_5, char_21);
  auto &char_27 = char_16;
  char_18 = std::exchange(char_16, char{'e'});
  auto &char_29 = char_6;
  print("{}{}{}{}{}{}",
        char_27, char_6, char_26, char_14, char_16, char_1);
}

// Answer (8):

// __ __ __ __ __ __ __ __
```

**Puzzle 122**

```
auto function(char &parameter_1, char &parameter_2) {
  char char_1{'l'};
  auto &char_2 = char_1;
  char_1 = 'x';
  auto &char_4 = parameter_2;
  char_1 = 'o';
  print("{}",
        parameter_1);
}
```

```
void run() {
  char char_1{'a'};
  auto char_2 = char_1;
  char_2 = 'r';
  auto char_4 = char_2;
  char_4 = 'i';
  char_4 = std::exchange(char_2, char{'a'});
  char char_7{'n'};
  auto char_8 = char_2;
  char_1 = '.';
  auto &char_10 = char_4;
  char char_11{'r'};
  auto char_12 = char_2;
  char char_13{'e'};
  function(char_11, char_2);
  char char_14{'m'};
  char_2 = std::exchange(char_1, char{'s'});
  auto char_16 = char_7;
  function(char_8, char_1);
  std::swap(char_10, char_16);
  char char_17{'d'};
  auto char_18 = char_1;
  print("{}{}{}{}{}",
        char_7, char_17, char_2, char_13, char_10);
  char_2 = 'h';
  auto &char_20 = char_2;
  auto char_21 = char_14;
  char char_22{'.'};
  auto char_23 = char_21;
  char_8 = 'r';
  char char_25{'e'};
  auto char_26 = char_10;
  char char_27{'g'};
  char_10 = 'r';
  auto &char_29 = char_8;
  print("{}{}{}{}{}{}",
        char_27, char_22, char_14, char_25, char_11, char_1);
}

// Answer (13):

// __ __ __ __ __ __ __ __ __ __ __ __ __
```

**Puzzle 123**

```
auto function(char parameter_1, char &parameter_2) {
  parameter_2 = 'e';
  parameter_2 = 'p';
  char char_3{'x'};
  auto char_4 = parameter_1;
  print("{}",
        char_3);
  auto &char_5 = char_4;
  print("{}",
        parameter_2);
}
void run() {
  char char_1{'e'};
  print("{}",
        char_1);
  auto &char_2 = char_1;
  char char_3{'x'};
  auto char_4 = char_3;
  auto &char_5 = char_2;
  char char_6{'c'};
  auto char_7 = char_4;
  char char_8{'d'};
  std::swap(char_6, char_1);
  auto &char_9 = char_5;
  char char_10{'c'};
  auto &char_11 = char_1;
  std::swap(char_11, char_6);
  char char_12{'m'};
  auto &char_13 = char_12;
  char char_14{'m'};
  char_3 = '.';
  auto char_16 = char_14;
  auto &char_17 = char_7;
  char_11 = std::exchange(char_10, char{'a'});
  auto &char_19 = char_8;
  char_6 = 'o';
  function(char_12, char_17);
  auto &char_21 = char_9;
  char char_22{'p'};
  char_17 = std::exchange(char_16, char{'j'});
  auto &char_24 = char_22;
```

```
  char_12 = 'r';
  char char_26{'y'};
  auto &char_27 = char_13;
  print("{}{}{}{}{}{}{}",
        char_13, char_3, char_11, char_6, char_17, char_14,
        char_10);
}

// Answer (10):

// __ __ __ __ __ __ __ __ __ __
```

**Puzzle 124**

```
auto function(char &parameter_1, char &parameter_2) {
  std::swap(parameter_2, parameter_1);
  parameter_2 = 'm';
  char char_2{'k'};
  std::swap(parameter_2, char_2);
  auto &char_3 = parameter_2;
  char char_4{'t'};
  print("{}",
        char_2);
}
void run() {
  char char_1{'m'};
  auto &char_2 = char_1;
  char_1 = 'g';
  char char_4{'y'};
  function(char_2, char_1);
  char_4 = std::exchange(char_1, char{'e'});
  char_4 = 'e';
  char char_7{'q'};
  auto &char_8 = char_1;
  print("{}",
        char_2);
  char_4 = 'v';
  auto &char_10 = char_7;
  char char_11{'n'};
  auto char_12 = char_11;
  char_10 = '.';
  char char_14{'y'};
  char_2 = std::exchange(char_11, char{'w'});
```

```
  auto char_16 = char_1;
  char_12 = 'r';
  auto char_18 = char_7;
  char_10 = 'a';
  auto char_20 = char_10;
  std::swap(char_12, char_11);
  auto &char_21 = char_16;
  auto char_22 = char_8;
  char_1 = 't';
  char char_24{'m'};
  auto &char_25 = char_14;
  auto char_26 = char_11;
  char char_27{'u'};
  char_16 = 'l';
  auto char_29 = char_26;
  char_16 = 'n';
  char char_31{'x'};
  char_31 = 't';
  char char_33{'k'};
  auto char_34 = char_27;
  print("{}{}{}{}{}{}{}{}",
        char_8, char_20, char_18, char_34, char_21, char_10,
        char_29, char_14);
}

// Answer (10):

// __ __ __ __ __ __ __ __ __ __
```

**Puzzle 125**

```
auto function(char &parameter_1, char parameter_2) {
  parameter_2 = std::exchange(parameter_1, char{'l'});
  char char_2{'y'};
  parameter_1 = 'W';
  std::swap(char_2, parameter_1);
  char char_4{'A'};
  print("{}{}",
        char_2, char_4);
}
void run() {
  char char_1{'e'};
  char char_2{'k'};
```

```
    char_2 = 'W';
    std::swap(char_2, char_1);
    char_2 = 'A';
    char_2 = std::exchange(char_1, char{'A'});
    print("{}",
          char_2);
    char char_6{'t'};
    auto &char_7 = char_2;
    char_7 = 'h';
    auto &char_9 = char_1;
    auto char_10 = char_1;
    char_7 = 'F';
    auto char_12 = char_6;
    char char_13{'/'};
    auto char_14 = char_13;
    std::swap(char_10, char_1);
    char_13 = 'I';
    auto char_16 = char_1;
    char_6 = std::exchange(char_1, char{'T'});
    auto &char_18 = char_7;
    print("{}{}{}{}{}",
          char_16, char_13, char_1, char_14, char_7);
    char char_19{'I'};
    auto &char_20 = char_10;
    char char_21{'a'};
    char_10 = 'i';
    auto char_23 = char_6;
    auto &char_24 = char_12;
    char_1 = '-';
    char char_26{'T'};
    function(char_14, char_24);
    char char_27{'i'};
    auto &char_28 = char_12;
    char char_29{'W'};
    auto char_30 = char_12;
    char char_31{'r'};
    auto &char_32 = char_1;
    print("{}{}{}{}{}{}{}",
          char_19, char_26, char_32, char_29, char_21, char_27,
          char_12);
}

// Answer (15):
```

```
// __ __ __ __ __ __ __ __ __ __ __ __ __ __ __
```

**Puzzle 126**

```
auto function(char &parameter_1, char &parameter_2) {
  parameter_2 = 'f';
  char char_2{'p'};
  parameter_1 = 'e';
  auto char_4 = char_2;
  std::swap(parameter_2, char_4);
  auto char_5 = parameter_2;
  print("{}",
        parameter_1);
}
void run() {
  char char_1{'n'};
  auto char_2 = char_1;
  char char_3{'e'};
  auto &char_4 = char_3;
  char_4 = std::exchange(char_3, char{'d'});
  auto char_6 = char_1;
  std::swap(char_6, char_2);
  char_6 = 'n';
  auto char_8 = char_3;
  char char_9{'t'};
  auto &char_10 = char_4;
  auto char_11 = char_6;
  char char_12{'q'};
  auto &char_13 = char_10;
  auto char_14 = char_11;
  char_2 = 'v';
  auto &char_16 = char_8;
  auto char_17 = char_16;
  std::swap(char_9, char_10);
  char char_18{'c'};
  char_6 = 'e';
  auto char_20 = char_8;
  char char_21{'x'};
  std::swap(char_2, char_3);
  char_10 = 'v';
  char char_23{'r'};
  char_13 = '.';
```

```
  auto char_25 = char_16;
  char char_26{'v'};
  auto &char_27 = char_11;
  function(char_27, char_9);
  auto &char_28 = char_27;
  char_16 = 'p';
  auto &char_30 = char_11;
  char_12 = 'q';
  auto &char_32 = char_23;
  print("{}{}{}{}{}{}{}{}{}{}",
        char_21, char_18, char_28, char_9, char_2, char_10,
        char_16, char_32, char_30);
}

// Answer (10):

// __ __ __ __ __ __ __ __ __ __
```

**Puzzle 127**

```
auto function(char parameter_1, char &parameter_2) {
  parameter_1 = 's';
  parameter_1 = std::exchange(parameter_2, char{'h'});
  std::swap(parameter_1, parameter_2);
  parameter_1 = 'u';
  char char_4{'t'};
  auto &char_5 = parameter_1;
  print("{}",
        char_5);
}
void run() {
  char char_1{'y'};
  auto char_2 = char_1;
  std::swap(char_1, char_2);
  char char_3{'u'};
  char_1 = 'd';
  char char_5{'i'};
  char_3 = 'c';
  auto &char_7 = char_3;
  std::swap(char_2, char_1);
  char_1 = std::exchange(char_2, char{'f'});
  auto &char_9 = char_2;
  char_3 = 'd';
```

```
    auto &char_11 = char_7;
    char_1 = 'a';
    auto char_13 = char_3;
    std::swap(char_13, char_9);
    char_2 = 'e';
    auto char_15 = char_1;
    char_3 = 'm';
    auto char_17 = char_2;
    char_11 = 'l';
    auto char_19 = char_5;
    char char_20{'v'};
    std::swap(char_7, char_19);
    char_2 = '.';
    auto &char_22 = char_7;
    char_3 = 'h';
    auto char_24 = char_5;
    char char_25{'n'};
    auto &char_26 = char_17;
    char_20 = 'b';
    auto &char_28 = char_15;
    char char_29{'y'};
    char_1 = 'd';
    auto &char_31 = char_11;
    std::swap(char_11, char_28);
    auto char_32 = char_15;
    std::swap(char_22, char_28);
    auto char_33 = char_31;
    function(char_19, char_5);
    auto &char_34 = char_33;
    char_3 = 'd';
    auto &char_36 = char_24;
    char_19 = 'a';
    char_19 = std::exchange(char_26, char{'d'});
    char char_39{'x'};
    print("{}{}{}{}{}{}{}{}{}",
          char_28, char_39, char_36, char_17, char_9, char_7,
          char_19, char_13);
}

// Answer (9):

// __ __ __ __ __ __ __ __ __
```

**Puzzle 128**

```
auto function(char &parameter_1, char parameter_2) {
  char char_1{'o'};
  std::swap(parameter_2, char_1);
  char_1 = 'l';
  parameter_1 = std::exchange(char_1, char{'.'});
  std::swap(parameter_1, char_1);
  char char_4{'a'};
  print("{}{}",
        char_1, parameter_2);
}
void run() {
  char char_1{'o'};
  auto &char_2 = char_1;
  char_2 = '.';
  char char_4{'a'};
  auto char_5 = char_4;
  function(char_2, char_4);
  auto &char_6 = char_2;
  char_6 = std::exchange(char_1, char{'w'});
  auto char_8 = char_6;
  char char_9{'j'};
  char_5 = 'a';
  std::swap(char_1, char_9);
  auto &char_11 = char_5;
  auto char_12 = char_8;
  char_5 = 'l';
  auto &char_14 = char_11;
  char_8 = 'e';
  auto &char_16 = char_9;
  char_6 = std::exchange(char_4, char{'e'});
  auto char_18 = char_8;
  char char_19{'f'};
  auto &char_20 = char_2;
  auto char_21 = char_16;
  char_21 = 't';
  char_21 = std::exchange(char_2, char{'b'});
  char_19 = 'c';
  auto &char_25 = char_16;
  auto char_26 = char_25;
  char char_27{'y'};
  auto &char_28 = char_26;
```

```
    char char_29{'l'};
    auto &char_30 = char_4;
    std::swap(char_5, char_21);
    char_20 = 'r';
    auto &char_32 = char_21;
    char char_33{'n'};
    std::swap(char_2, char_20);
    auto &char_34 = char_4;
    char_25 = 'c';
    char_26 = std::exchange(char_20, char{'l'});
    char_9 = 'g';
    char char_38{'e'};
    print("{}{}{}{}{}{}{}{}{}{}{}{}{}{}",
          char_19, char_5, char_32, char_18, char_12, char_16,
          char_30, char_33, char_4, char_28, char_14, char_29);
}

// Answer (14):

// __ __ __ __ __ __ __ __ __ __ __ __ __ __
```

# Solutions

**Solution 1**

```
void run() {
  char char_1{'q'};
  char_1 = 'm';
  char char_3{'j'};
  char_1 = 'v';
  char char_5{'a'};
  char_5 = 'q';
  char char_7{'c'};
  char_7 = 'w';
  char char_9{'s'};
  print("{}{}",                              // ws
        char_7, char_9);
}

// Answer: ws
```

**Solution 2**

```
void run() {
  char char_1{'g'};
  char char_2{'c'};
  char_2 = 'w';
  char char_4{'v'};
  char_1 = 'v';
  char char_6{'r'};
  char_2 = 'e';
  char char_8{'o'};
  print("{}{}",                              // or
        char_8, char_6);
}

// Answer: or
```

**Solution 3**

```
void run() {
  char char_1{'c'};
  char_1 = 'x';
  char char_3{'f'};
  char_3 = 'd';
  char char_5{'q'};
  char_1 = 'a';
  char char_7{'v'};
  char_7 = 'e';
  char char_9{'e'};
  char_3 = 'x';
  char char_11{'e'};
  print("{}{}{}",                                  // exa
        char_9, char_3, char_1);
}

// Answer: exa
```

**Solution 4**

```
void run() {
  char char_1{'n'};
  char_1 = 'h';
  char char_3{'j'};
  char_1 = 'l';
  char char_5{'f'};
  char_3 = 'i';
  char char_7{'y'};
  char_7 = 'j';
  char char_9{'e'};
  char_1 = 'n';
  char char_11{'y'};
  print("{}{}",                                    // in
        char_3, char_1);
}

// Answer: in
```

**Solution 5**

```
void run() {
  char char_1{'m'};
  char_1 = 'c';
  char char_3{'l'};
  char_3 = 's';
  char char_5{'q'};
  char_5 = 'u';
  char char_7{'s'};
  char_5 = 'a';
  char char_9{'t'};
  char_7 = 'k';
  char char_11{'r'};
  char_1 = 'e';
  char char_13{'w'};
  print("{}{}{}{}",                          // setw
        char_3, char_1, char_9, char_13);
}

// Answer: setw
```

**Solution 6**

```
void run() {
  char char_1{'t'};
  char_1 = 'q';
  char char_3{'l'};
  char_1 = 'g';
  char char_5{'q'};
  char_1 = 'l';
  char char_7{'m'};
  char_3 = 'v';
  char char_9{'k'};
  char_1 = 'c';
  char char_11{'l'};
  char_9 = 'e';
  char char_13{'n'};
  print("{}{}{}",                            // lcm
        char_11, char_1, char_7);
}

// Answer: lcm
```

**Solution 7**

```
void run() {
  char char_1{'u'};
  char_1 = 'g';
  char char_3{'j'};
  char_3 = 't';
  char char_5{'u'};
  char_3 = 'n';
  char char_7{'r'};
  char_5 = 'f';
  char char_9{'r'};
  char_5 = 'w';
  char char_11{'g'};
  char_1 = 'j';
  char char_13{'o'};
  char_1 = 'w';
  char char_15{'m'};
  print("{}{}{}{}",                                   // norm
        char_3, char_13, char_7, char_15);
}

// Answer: norm
```

**Solution 8**

```
void run() {
  char char_1{'j'};
  char char_2{'v'};
  char_2 = 'p';
  char char_4{'l'};
  char_1 = 'i';
  char char_6{'g'};
  char_2 = 'c';
  char char_8{'i'};
  char_8 = 'q';
  char char_10{'m'};
  char_1 = 'o';
  char char_12{'i'};
  char_1 = 't';
  char char_14{'e'};
  print("{}{}{}{}",                                   // ceil
        char_2, char_14, char_12, char_4);
```

```
}

// Answer: ceil
```

**Solution 9**

```
void run() {
  char char_1{'a'};
  char_1 = 'R';
  char char_3{'u'};
  auto char_4 = char_1;
  char_3 = 'C';
  auto char_6 = char_4;
  char char_7{'i'};
  print("{}{}{}",                                  // RCR
        char_6, char_3, char_4);
}

// Answer: RCR
```

**Solution 10**

```
void run() {
  char char_1{'a'};
  auto char_2 = char_1;
  char_2 = 'x';
  auto char_4 = char_1;
  char_1 = 'h';
  auto char_6 = char_1;
  char char_7{'e'};
  print("{}{}{}",                                  // hex
        char_1, char_7, char_2);
}

// Answer: hex
```

**Solution 11**

```
void run() {
  char char_1{'v'};
  auto char_2 = char_1;
  char char_3{'s'};
  char_2 = 'm';
  char char_5{'d'};
  char_5 = 'b';
  auto char_7 = char_3;
  char char_8{'a'};
  print("{}{}{}",                          // asm
        char_8, char_3, char_2);
}

// Answer: asm
```

**Solution 12**

```
void run() {
  char char_1{'h'};
  char_1 = 'R';
  auto char_3 = char_1;
  char_3 = 'd';
  char char_5{'s'};
  char_5 = 'C';
  char char_7{'q'};
  char_7 = 'c';
  char char_9{'L'};
  char_3 = 'g';
  auto char_11 = char_5;
  print("{}{}{}",                          // RCL
        char_1, char_11, char_9);
}

// Answer: RCL
```

**Solution 13**

```
void run() {
  char char_1{'r'};
  char_1 = 'a';
  char char_3{'a'};
  char_1 = 'i';
  auto char_5 = char_1;
  char char_6{'n'};
  auto char_7 = char_1;
  char_1 = 'a';
  char char_9{'w'};
  auto char_10 = char_6;
  print("{}{}{}",                              // nan
        char_10, char_3, char_6);
}

// Answer: nan
```

**Solution 14**

```
void run() {
  char char_1{'o'};
  char_1 = 'u';
  auto char_3 = char_1;
  char_1 = 'p';
  char char_5{'t'};
  auto char_6 = char_1;
  char_1 = 'm';
  auto char_8 = char_6;
  char char_9{'l'};
  char_1 = 'o';
  auto char_11 = char_1;
  print("{}{}{}",                              // out
        char_1, char_3, char_5);
}

// Answer: out
```

**Solution 15**

```
void run() {
  char char_1{'l'};
  auto char_2 = char_1;
  char char_3{'e'};
  char_1 = 'q';
  char char_5{'y'};
  auto char_6 = char_2;
  char_5 = 'b';
  char char_8{'r'};
  auto char_9 = char_2;
  char_6 = 'p';
  auto char_11 = char_5;
  print("{}{}{}{}",                                   // lerp
        char_2, char_3, char_8, char_6);
}

// Answer: lerp
```

**Solution 16**

```
void run() {
  char char_1{'f'};
  char_1 = 't';
  auto char_3 = char_1;
  char char_4{'o'};
  auto char_5 = char_4;
  char char_6{'g'};
  char_3 = 'u';
  char char_8{'v'};
  auto char_9 = char_4;
  char_3 = 'g';
  auto char_11 = char_8;
  print("{}{}{}{}",                                   // goto
        char_6, char_4, char_1, char_9);
}

// Answer: goto
```

**Solution 17**

```
void run() {
  char char_1{'u'};
  char_1 = 'h';
  auto &char_3 = char_1;
  char_1 = 'n';
  auto &char_5 = char_1;
  char_3 = 't';
  char char_7{'s'};
  char_5 = 'w';
  auto &char_9 = char_3;
  print("{}",                                          // w
        char_5);
}

// Answer: w
```

**Solution 18**

```
void run() {
  char char_1{'y'};
  auto &char_2 = char_1;
  char char_3{'t'};
  char_1 = 'm';
  auto &char_5 = char_1;
  char char_6{'e'};
  print("{}{}",                                        // tm
        char_3, char_5);
}

// Answer: tm
```

**Solution 19**

```
void run() {
  char char_1{'c'};
  char_1 = 't';
  auto &char_3 = char_1;
  char char_4{'e'};
  auto &char_5 = char_1;
  char char_6{'g'};
  auto &char_7 = char_4;
```

```
  print("{}{}{}",                             // get
        char_6, char_7, char_1);
}

// Answer: get
```

**Solution 20**

```
void run() {
  char char_1{'y'};
  char_1 = 'b';
  char char_3{'p'};
  char_3 = 'o';
  char char_5{'y'};
  auto &char_6 = char_5;
  char_6 = 'w';
  auto &char_8 = char_3;
  char char_9{'l'};
  print("{}{}{}{}",                           // bool
        char_1, char_3, char_8, char_9);
}

// Answer: bool
```

**Solution 21**

```
void run() {
  char char_1{'n'};
  char_1 = 'g';
  auto &char_3 = char_1;
  char char_4{'l'};
  auto &char_5 = char_4;
  char char_6{'c'};
  auto &char_7 = char_1;
  char_4 = 'd';
  auto &char_9 = char_3;
  print("{}{}{}",                             // gcd
        char_9, char_6, char_5);
}

// Answer: gcd
```

**Solution 22**

```
void run() {
  char char_1{'d'};
  char char_2{'i'};
  auto &char_3 = char_1;
  char char_4{'s'};
  char_3 = 'j';
  auto &char_6 = char_4;
  char char_7{'l'};
  auto &char_8 = char_6;
  print("{}{}",                                    // is
        char_2, char_4);
}

// Answer: is
```

**Solution 23**

```
void run() {
  char char_1{'k'};
  auto &char_2 = char_1;
  char char_3{'k'};
  auto &char_4 = char_3;
  char char_5{'f'};
  char_5 = 'm';
  auto &char_7 = char_3;
  char_3 = 'a';
  char char_9{'g'};
  char_1 = 'm';
  auto &char_11 = char_2;
  print("{}{}{}{}{}",                              // gamma
        char_9, char_3, char_2, char_5, char_7);
}

// Answer: gamma
```

**Solution 24**

```
void run() {
  char char_1{'q'};
  auto &char_2 = char_1;
  char char_3{'f'};
  auto &char_4 = char_2;
  char char_5{'l'};
  char_3 = 'e';
  char char_7{'x'};
  char_3 = 'r';
  auto &char_9 = char_4;
  char_4 = 'o';
  char char_11{'l'};
  print("{}{}{}",                              // xor
        char_7, char_1, char_3);
}

// Answer: xor
```

**Solution 25**

```
void run() {
  char char_1{'A'};
  auto char_2 = char_1;
  char char_3{'w'};
  auto char_4 = char_1;
  auto &char_5 = char_2;
  char_4 = 'D';
  char char_7{'P'};
  print("{}{}",                                // PA
        char_7, char_1);
  char char_8{'D'};
  auto &char_9 = char_8;
  auto char_10 = char_9;
  auto &char_11 = char_2;
  print("{}{}{}",                              // DDD
        char_4, char_10, char_9);
}

// Answer: PADDD
```

**Solution 26**

```
void run() {
  char char_1{'g'};
  char_1 = 'f';
  print("{}",                                     // f
        char_1);
  auto &char_3 = char_1;
  auto char_4 = char_1;
  auto &char_5 = char_4;
  char char_6{'v'};
  char_3 = 'h';
  auto char_8 = char_6;
  char_1 = 'o';
  auto &char_10 = char_1;
  char_6 = 'r';
  char char_12{'l'};
  auto char_13 = char_4;
  char_4 = 'l';
  char char_15{'y'};
  print("{}{}{}{}{}",                             // loorl
        char_5, char_10, char_3, char_6, char_4);
}

// Answer: floorl
```

**Solution 27**

```
void run() {
  char char_1{'q'};
  char_1 = 'f';
  auto char_3 = char_1;
  char char_4{'i'};
  auto &char_5 = char_4;
  char_4 = 'y';
  auto &char_7 = char_5;
  auto char_8 = char_5;
  auto &char_9 = char_8;
  char_5 = 'e';
  auto &char_11 = char_3;
  char_8 = 'k';
  char char_13{'s'};
  auto char_14 = char_9;
```

```
  print("{}{}{}{}{}",                          // fseek
        char_11, char_13, char_4, char_7, char_8);
}

// Answer: fseek
```

**Solution 28**

```
void run() {
  char char_1{'a'};
  char_1 = 'y';
  auto char_3 = char_1;
  auto &char_4 = char_1;
  char_1 = 'c';
  char char_6{'u'};
  auto char_7 = char_3;
  auto &char_8 = char_1;
  char char_9{'a'};
  char_7 = 'v';
  print("{}{}{}",                              // cau
        char_8, char_9, char_6);
  auto char_11 = char_9;
  char char_12{'h'};
  auto char_13 = char_8;
  print("{}{}{}",                              // chy
        char_13, char_12, char_3);
}

// Answer: cauchy
```

**Solution 29**

```
void run() {
  char char_1{'t'};
  auto &char_2 = char_1;
  char char_3{'c'};
  auto char_4 = char_1;
  char_4 = 'g';
  char char_6{'l'};
  auto &char_7 = char_4;
  char char_8{'d'};
  char_8 = 'r';
  auto char_10 = char_3;
```

```
  char_7 = 'b';
  char char_12{'e'};
  auto char_13 = char_8;
  auto &char_14 = char_13;
  print("{}{}{}{}{}",                         // cbrtl
        char_3, char_4, char_8, char_1, char_6);
}

// Answer: cbrtl
```

**Solution 30**

```
void run() {
  char char_1{'e'};
  auto char_2 = char_1;
  char_1 = 'd';
  auto char_4 = char_1;
  char_4 = 'j';
  char char_6{'e'};
  print("{}{}",                               // de
        char_1, char_6);
  char_1 = 'w';
  auto &char_8 = char_4;
  char char_9{'l'};
  auto char_10 = char_6;
  auto &char_11 = char_2;
  char char_12{'t'};
  auto &char_13 = char_1;
  char char_14{'r'};
  print("{}{}{}{}",                           // lete
        char_9, char_11, char_12, char_2);
}

// Answer: delete
```

**Solution 31**

```
void run() {
  char char_1{'c'};
  auto char_2 = char_1;
  print("{}",                                        // c
        char_1);
  auto &char_3 = char_2;
  char_2 = 'o';
  auto char_5 = char_3;
  char char_6{'n'};
  auto char_7 = char_2;
  char char_8{'m'};
  auto char_9 = char_5;
  auto &char_10 = char_8;
  char char_11{'n'};
  auto &char_12 = char_8;
  print("{}{}{}{}{}",                                // ommon
        char_9, char_10, char_12, char_5, char_11);
}

// Answer: common
```

**Solution 32**

```
void run() {
  char char_1{'H'};
  auto char_2 = char_1;
  char char_3{'D'};
  char_2 = 'A';
  auto &char_5 = char_2;
  auto char_6 = char_1;
  char char_7{'h'};
  auto char_8 = char_3;
  char_6 = 'D';
  char char_10{'P'};
  auto char_11 = char_2;
  char char_12{'i'};
  auto char_13 = char_1;
  print("{}{}{}{}{}{}",                              // PHADDD
        char_10, char_1, char_11, char_8, char_3, char_6);
}

// Answer: PHADDD
```

**Solution 33**

```
void run() {
  char char_1{'o'};
  char char_2{'f'};
  char_1 = 'i';
  auto &char_4 = char_2;
  auto char_5 = char_4;
  print("{}",                                    // f
        char_4);
  char char_6{'p'};
  auto char_7 = char_5;
  auto &char_8 = char_2;
  auto char_9 = char_1;
  char_9 = 'm';
  auto &char_11 = char_6;
  auto char_12 = char_7;
  char char_13{'a'};
  print("{}{}{}",                                // maf
        char_9, char_13, char_2);
}

// Answer: fmaf
```

**Solution 34**

```
void run() {
  char char_1{'j'};
  char_1 = 's';
  auto char_3 = char_1;
  char char_4{'i'};
  char_1 = 'l';
  print("{}{}",                                  // is
        char_4, char_3);
  char_4 = 'o';
  auto char_7 = char_3;
  char char_8{'x'};
  print("{}",                                    // l
        char_1);
  char_4 = 't';
  auto char_10 = char_3;
  auto &char_11 = char_4;
  char_4 = 'e';
```

```
  char char_13{'b'};
  auto char_14 = char_8;
  auto &char_15 = char_7;
  char char_16{'t'};
  print("{}{}{}",                          // ess
        char_11, char_10, char_15);
}

// Answer: isless
```

**Solution 35**

```
void run() {
  char char_1{'H'};
  auto char_2 = char_1;
  auto &char_3 = char_1;
  auto char_4 = char_3;
  char_1 = 'y';
  auto &char_6 = char_1;
  auto char_7 = char_6;
  char char_8{'d'};
  char_8 = 'S';
  char char_10{'U'};
  char_1 = 'f';
  auto &char_12 = char_2;
  char_6 = 'A';
  char char_14{'P'};
  auto &char_15 = char_6;
  auto char_16 = char_10;
  print("{}{}{}{}{}",                      // PUSHA
        char_14, char_10, char_8, char_4, char_3);
}

// Answer: PUSHA
```

**Solution 36**

```
void run() {
  char char_1{'i'};
  char_1 = 's';
  auto &char_3 = char_1;
  char char_4{'k'};
  char_4 = 'k';
  auto char_6 = char_3;
  auto &char_7 = char_4;
  char_6 = 'j';
  auto char_9 = char_1;
  char char_10{'m'};
  char_1 = 'e';
  char char_12{'r'};
  char_10 = 'a';
  auto &char_14 = char_12;
  char_4 = 'p';
  auto &char_16 = char_4;
  char char_17{'g'};
  char_10 = 'o';
  char char_19{'r'};
  print("{}{}{}{}{}{}",                          // perror
        char_16, char_1, char_14, char_19, char_10, char_12);
}

// Answer: perror
```

**Solution 37**

```
void run() {
  char char_1{'x'};
  char_1 = 'f';
  char char_3{'l'};
  char_1 = 'l';
  auto &char_5 = char_1;
  char_3 = 'w';
  char char_7{'e'};
  char_5 = 'n';
  auto char_9 = char_7;
  char char_10{'p'};
  auto &char_11 = char_7;
  auto char_12 = char_5;
```

```
  char char_13{'c'};
  char_12 = 'x';
  char char_15{'t'};
  char_13 = 'g';
  auto char_17 = char_10;
  auto &char_18 = char_15;
  print("{}{}{}{}{}{}",                             // extent
        char_9, char_12, char_15, char_11, char_1, char_18);
}

// Answer: extent
```

**Solution 38**

```
void run() {
  char char_1{'l'};
  auto &char_2 = char_1;
  auto char_3 = char_1;
  print("{}{}",                                     // ll
        char_1, char_2);
  auto char_4 = char_2;
  char char_5{'s'};
  auto char_6 = char_2;
  char char_7{'d'};
  char_4 = 'x';
  char char_9{'_'};
  auto char_10 = char_9;
  char char_11{'t'};
  char_6 = 'v';
  char char_13{'i'};
  auto char_14 = char_9;
  print("{}{}{}{}{}",                               // div_t
        char_7, char_13, char_6, char_9, char_11);
}

// Answer: lldiv_t
```

**Solution 39**

```
void run() {
  char char_1{'w'};
  auto &char_2 = char_1;
  auto char_3 = char_1;
  char_2 = 'f';
  auto &char_5 = char_2;
  auto char_6 = char_5;
  auto &char_7 = char_1;
  char_6 = 's';
  auto &char_9 = char_5;
  char_7 = 'c';
  auto &char_11 = char_1;
  print("{}{}{}",                              // wcs
        char_3, char_7, char_6);
  char char_12{'o'};
  auto &char_13 = char_7;
  char_5 = 'r';
  char char_15{'t'};
  auto &char_16 = char_6;
  print("{}{}{}",                              // str
        char_16, char_15, char_9);
}

// Answer: wcsstr
```

**Solution 40**

```
void run() {
  char char_1{'v'};
  char_1 = 'a';
  auto char_3 = char_1;
  char char_4{'b'};
  auto char_5 = char_1;
  char_1 = 'p';
  auto char_7 = char_5;
  char_5 = 'q';
  auto char_9 = char_4;
  char char_10{'e'};
  auto &char_11 = char_7;
  auto char_12 = char_4;
  char char_13{'t'};
```

```
  char_3 = 'e';
  auto char_15 = char_7;
  auto &char_16 = char_11;
  print("{}{}{}{}",                             // beta
        char_9, char_3, char_13, char_15);
}

// Answer: beta
```

**Solution 41**

```
void run() {
  char char_1{'m'};
  print("{}",                                   // m
        char_1);
  char_1 = 'b';
  char char_3{'x'};
  char_3 = 'a';
  auto &char_5 = char_3;
  print("{}",                                   // a
        char_3);
  char_3 = 'k';
  print("{}",                                   // k
        char_5);
  char_3 = 'y';
  char char_8{'e'};
  print("{}",                                   // e
        char_8);
  auto &char_9 = char_5;
  char char_10{'p'};
  char_8 = 'f';
  auto char_12 = char_3;
  char_3 = 'j';
  auto char_14 = char_3;
  char_14 = 'x';
  char char_16{'n'};
  char_14 = 'n';
  char char_18{'w'};
  char_14 = '_';
  auto char_20 = char_14;
  char char_21{'a'};
  char_18 = 'q';
  auto char_23 = char_5;
```

```
  print("{}{}{}{}",                               // _any
        char_20, char_21, char_16, char_12);
}

// Answer: make_any
```

**Solution 42**

```
void run() {
  char char_1{'l'};
  auto &char_2 = char_1;
  print("{}",                                     // l
        char_2);
  char_2 = 'n';
  auto &char_4 = char_1;
  char_1 = 'o';
  print("{}",                                     // o
        char_4);
  char char_6{'2'};
  auto &char_7 = char_4;
  char char_8{'f'};
  char_1 = 'm';
  auto char_10 = char_2;
  char char_11{'g'};
  char_1 = 'r';
  char char_13{'f'};
  auto char_14 = char_13;
  char char_15{'l'};
  auto char_16 = char_11;
  auto &char_17 = char_15;
  print("{}{}{}",                                 // g2l
        char_16, char_6, char_15);
}

// Answer: log2l
```

**Solution 43**

```
void run() {
  char char_1{'f'};
  auto &char_2 = char_1;
  print("{}",                                           // f
        char_1);
  char char_3{'c'};
  char_3 = 'r';
  char char_5{'q'};
  char_5 = 'w';
  char char_7{'c'};
  char_2 = 'r';
  auto &char_9 = char_3;
  auto char_10 = char_7;
  auto &char_11 = char_10;
  char_9 = 'h';
  auto &char_13 = char_10;
  char_10 = 'r';
  char char_15{'o'};
  auto char_16 = char_11;
  char char_17{'e'};
  char_3 = 'o';
  auto &char_19 = char_10;
  print("{}{}{}{}{}",                                   // error
        char_17, char_2, char_10, char_9, char_11);
}

// Answer: ferror
```

**Solution 44**

```
void run() {
  char char_1{'D'};
  char char_2{'u'};
  char_2 = 'K';
  auto char_4 = char_1;
  char char_5{'u'};
  auto char_6 = char_1;
  auto &char_7 = char_1;
  char char_8{'A'};
  auto char_9 = char_7;
  char_5 = 's';
```

```
  auto char_11 = char_8;
  char_6 = 'd';
  auto char_13 = char_4;
  auto &char_14 = char_1;
  char char_15{'h'};
  auto &char_16 = char_1;
  print("{}{}{}{}{}",                              // KADDD
        char_2, char_8, char_16, char_14, char_4);
}

// Answer: KADDD
```

**Solution 45**

```
void run() {
  char char_1{'n'};
  auto &char_2 = char_1;
  char char_3{'P'};
  char_1 = 'R';
  char char_5{'R'};
  auto &char_6 = char_1;
  print("{}{}",                                    // PR
        char_3, char_2);
  auto &char_7 = char_2;
  auto char_8 = char_2;
  char_8 = 'D';
  char char_10{'O'};
  auto char_11 = char_1;
  char_6 = 'V';
  char char_13{'m'};
  auto char_14 = char_10;
  char char_15{'b'};
  char_3 = 'w';
  auto char_17 = char_2;
  print("{}{}{}{}",                                // ORVD
        char_10, char_5, char_7, char_8);
}

// Answer: PRORVD
```

**Solution 46**

```
void run() {
  char char_1{'j'};
  auto &char_2 = char_1;
  char_1 = 'd';
  char char_4{'b'};
  char_2 = 'l';
  char char_6{'c'};
  auto char_7 = char_6;
  print("{}{}",                                    // cl
        char_7, char_2);
  auto char_8 = char_7;
  auto &char_9 = char_8;
  char_6 = 'o';
  auto &char_11 = char_2;
  char char_12{'k'};
  auto char_13 = char_7;
  char_9 = '_';
  char char_15{'r'};
  char_1 = 't';
  auto &char_17 = char_8;
  auto char_18 = char_7;
  print("{}{}{}{}{}",                              // ock_t
        char_6, char_18, char_12, char_8, char_11);
}

// Answer: clock_t
```

**Solution 47**

```
void run() {
  char char_1{'o'};
  char_1 = 'w';
  auto &char_3 = char_1;
  char_3 = 'c';
  char char_5{'x'};
  auto &char_6 = char_5;
  auto char_7 = char_3;
  auto &char_8 = char_6;
  char char_9{'a'};
  auto &char_10 = char_9;
  auto char_11 = char_6;
```

```
  char_1 = 'f';
  char char_13{'n'};
  auto &char_14 = char_5;
  char_8 = 's';
  char char_16{'c'};
  auto &char_17 = char_14;
  char char_18{'v'};
  print("{}{}{}{}{}{}{}",                             // vsscanf
        char_18, char_17, char_14, char_7, char_10, char_13,
        char_1);
}

// Answer: vsscanf
```

**Solution 48**

```
void run() {
  char char_1{'D'};
  print("{}",                                         // D
        char_1);
  char char_2{'r'};
  auto char_3 = char_2;
  auto &char_4 = char_3;
  auto char_5 = char_1;
  auto &char_6 = char_3;
  char char_7{'i'};
  char_3 = 'd';
  char char_9{'e'};
  char_5 = 'i';
  auto char_11 = char_3;
  char_7 = 'k';
  auto char_13 = char_5;
  char_2 = 'v';
  char char_15{'x'};
  auto &char_16 = char_13;
  char char_17{'m'};
  auto char_18 = char_15;
  print("{}{}{}{}{}",                                 // ivide
        char_5, char_2, char_16, char_11, char_9);
}

// Answer: Divide
```

**Solution 49**

```
void run() {
  char char_1{'M'};
  print("{}",                                         // M
        char_1);
  auto &char_2 = char_1;
  auto char_3 = char_1;
  char_2 = 'n';
  auto &char_5 = char_2;
  char char_6{'D'};
  auto char_7 = char_6;
  char char_8{'f'};
  auto char_9 = char_7;
  char_9 = 'x';
  auto char_11 = char_5;
  char char_12{'S'};
  auto &char_13 = char_9;
  char char_14{'v'};
  char_5 = 'V';
  char char_16{'X'};
  char_9 = 'O';
  auto char_18 = char_6;
  print("{}{}{}{}{}",                                 // OVSXD
        char_9, char_2, char_12, char_16, char_18);
}

// Answer: MOVSXD
```

**Solution 50**

```
void run() {
  char char_1{'u'};
  char char_2{'r'};
  auto &char_3 = char_2;
  char_3 = 'o';
  auto &char_5 = char_1;
  print("{}",                                         // o
        char_3);
  char char_6{'t'};
  auto char_7 = char_5;
  auto &char_8 = char_3;
  char char_9{'_'};
```

```
  char_2 = 't';
  char char_11{'t'};
  auto &char_12 = char_8;
  auto char_13 = char_1;
  print("{}{}{}",                              // ut_
        char_13, char_12, char_9);
  char_1 = 'r';
  char char_15{'p'};
  auto char_16 = char_6;
  char_7 = 'e';
  char char_18{'_'};
  print("{}{}{}{}{}",                          // ptr_t
        char_15, char_8, char_5, char_18, char_11);
}

// Answer: out_ptr_t
```

**Solution 51**

```
void run() {
  char char_1{'r'};
  char_1 = 'i';
  auto char_3 = char_1;
  auto &char_4 = char_3;
  char char_5{'e'};
  auto char_6 = char_1;
  char char_7{'m'};
  char_6 = 'c';
  auto char_9 = char_4;
  char_1 = 'i';
  auto char_11 = char_1;
  char_11 = 'r';
  auto char_13 = char_5;
  auto &char_14 = char_13;
  auto char_15 = char_11;
  char char_16{'l'};
  char_4 = 'r';
  char char_18{'a'};
  auto &char_19 = char_3;
  print("{}{}{}{}{}{}{}{}",                    // clearerr
        char_6, char_16, char_5, char_18, char_4, char_13,
        char_15, char_3);
}
```

```
// Answer: clearerr
```

**Solution 52**

```
void run() {
  char char_1{'m'};
  auto char_2 = char_1;
  auto &char_3 = char_1;
  print("{}",                                    // m
        char_3);
  char_2 = 'g';
  auto char_5 = char_1;
  char_5 = 'f';
  auto &char_7 = char_1;
  auto char_8 = char_3;
  char_5 = 'p';
  char char_10{'c'};
  auto &char_11 = char_2;
  auto char_12 = char_7;
  auto &char_13 = char_3;
  auto char_14 = char_5;
  char char_15{'q'};
  auto char_16 = char_7;
  char_11 = 'e';
  auto &char_18 = char_15;
  print("{}{}{}{}{}",                            // emcmp
        char_2, char_1, char_10, char_8, char_14);
}

// Answer: memcmp
```

**Solution 53**

```
void run() {
  char char_1{'r'};
  auto char_2 = char_1;
  auto &char_3 = char_1;
  auto char_4 = char_1;
  char_3 = 'r';
  char char_6{'p'};
  auto char_7 = char_3;
  char char_8{'o'};
```

```
  auto char_9 = char_4;
  auto &char_10 = char_6;
  char char_11{'p'};
  auto &char_12 = char_10;
  char_9 = 't';
  auto char_14 = char_8;
  char_11 = 'e';
  auto &char_16 = char_3;
  auto char_17 = char_4;
  char char_18{'g'};
  print("{}{}{}{}{}",                               // error
        char_11, char_4, char_1, char_14, char_2);
}

// Answer: error
```

**Solution 54**

```
void run() {
  char char_1{'p'};
  auto char_2 = char_1;
  auto &char_3 = char_2;
  char_3 = 'h';
  char char_5{'u'};
  auto &char_6 = char_5;
  char char_7{'y'};
  auto char_8 = char_1;
  char_6 = 'r';
  char char_10{'o'};
  auto &char_11 = char_3;
  char char_12{'m'};
  char_12 = 'i';
  auto &char_14 = char_7;
  char_8 = 'b';
  auto &char_16 = char_5;
  auto char_17 = char_12;
  char_8 = 'h';
  auto &char_19 = char_8;
  char_8 = 'm';
  char char_21{'t'};
  print("{}{}{}{}{}{}",                             // import
        char_12, char_19, char_1, char_10, char_16, char_21);
}
```

```
// Answer: import
```

**Solution 55**

```
void run() {
  char char_1{'a'};
  auto char_2 = char_1;
  char char_3{'r'};
  auto &char_4 = char_2;
  auto char_5 = char_4;
  char_1 = 'c';
  char char_7{'e'};
  auto char_8 = char_7;
  char_4 = 'm';
  print("{}{}{}",                                  // mer
        char_4, char_8, char_3);
  char char_10{'l'};
  auto &char_11 = char_2;
  char_4 = 'b';
  char char_13{'g'};
  auto &char_14 = char_10;
  auto char_15 = char_3;
  auto &char_16 = char_8;
  char char_17{'l'};
  auto &char_18 = char_15;
  print("{}{}{}{}{}{}",                            // geable
        char_13, char_16, char_5, char_2, char_17, char_7);
}

// Answer: mergeable
```

**Solution 56**

```
void run() {
  char char_1{'s'};
  auto char_2 = char_1;
  auto &char_3 = char_1;
  auto char_4 = char_1;
  auto &char_5 = char_1;
  char_1 = 'i';
  auto char_7 = char_2;
  char_4 = 'h';
```

```
  char char_9{'m'};
  auto &char_10 = char_2;
  char char_11{'g'};
  auto &char_12 = char_5;
  auto char_13 = char_4;
  char char_14{'t'};
  auto char_15 = char_10;
  char_9 = 'w';
  char char_17{'x'};
  char_10 = 'd';
  auto &char_19 = char_14;
  print("{}{}{}{}{}{}{}{}{}",                         // iswxdigit
        char_5, char_15, char_9, char_17, char_2, char_3,
        char_11, char_1, char_19);
}

// Answer: iswxdigit
```

**Solution 57**

```
auto function(char parameter_1, char &parameter_2) {
  char char_1{'s'};
  auto char_2 = parameter_1;
  char_1 = 'r';
  char char_4{'a'};
  auto char_5 = char_1;
  parameter_2 = 'm';
  print("{}{}",
        parameter_1, char_1);
}
void run() {
  char char_1{'s'};
  auto char_2 = char_1;
  char char_3{'r'};
  char_3 = 'a';
  auto char_5 = char_2;
  char_2 = 'm';
  char char_7{'r'};
  print("{}",                                         // s
        char_5);
  auto char_8 = char_7;
  auto &char_9 = char_7;
  char_8 = 'i';
```

```
  auto &char_11 = char_5;
  char char_12{'t'};
  print("{}{}{}",                                    // trs
        char_12, char_7, char_1);
  function(char_12, char_11);                        // tr
  char_7 = 'e';
  auto char_14 = char_5;
  print("{}{}{}",                                    // eam
        char_9, char_3, char_14);
}

// Answer: strstream
```

**Solution 58**

```
auto function(char &parameter_1, char &parameter_2) {
  char char_1{'s'};
  parameter_1 = 'a';
  print("{}",
        char_1);
  char char_3{'m'};
  auto char_4 = char_3;
  print("{}{}",
        parameter_1, char_3);
}
void run() {
  char char_1{'s'};
  char char_2{'a'};
  function(char_1, char_2);                          // s
                                                     // am
  char_2 = 'm';
  auto &char_4 = char_2;
  char char_5{'l'};
  auto &char_6 = char_2;
  char char_7{'p'};
  auto char_8 = char_5;
  char_2 = 'e';
  char char_10{'l'};
  auto &char_11 = char_4;
  auto char_12 = char_6;
  print("{}{}{}",                                    // ple
        char_7, char_5, char_6);
}
```

```
// Answer: sample
```

**Solution 59**

```
auto function(char &parameter_1, char &parameter_2) {
  parameter_2 = 'a';
  parameter_1 = 'o';
  print("{}",
        parameter_2);
  char char_3{'m'};
  auto &char_4 = parameter_2;
  parameter_2 = 'c';
  print("{}{}",
        char_4, parameter_1);
}
void run() {
  char char_1{'a'};
  auto char_2 = char_1;
  char_2 = 'k';
  char char_4{'f'};
  char_4 = 'c';
  char char_6{'s'};
  function(char_4, char_1);                       // a
                                                  // co
  char_1 = 'e';
  auto char_8 = char_2;
  char_8 = 'l';
  auto char_10 = char_1;
  char_2 = 'g';
  auto char_12 = char_4;
  auto &char_13 = char_6;
  char char_14{'x'};
  auto char_15 = char_10;
  char char_16{'h'};
  print("{}{}{}",                                 // shl
        char_13, char_16, char_8);
}

// Answer: acoshl
```

**Solution 60**

```
auto function(char &parameter_1, char &parameter_2) {
  char char_1{'m'};
  char_1 = 'n';
  auto &char_3 = char_1;
  auto char_4 = parameter_2;
  char_4 = 'e';
  auto char_6 = char_4;
  print("{}{}",
        parameter_1, char_6);
}
void run() {
  char char_1{'m'};
  char char_2{'n'};
  function(char_1, char_2);                          // me
  auto &char_3 = char_2;
  auto char_4 = char_3;
  char_1 = 'e';
  char char_6{'r'};
  char_1 = 'u';
  print("{}",                                        // r
        char_6);
  char_3 = 'x';
  auto &char_9 = char_1;
  char char_10{'s'};
  char_9 = 'e';
  char char_12{'n'};
  auto &char_13 = char_1;
  auto char_14 = char_3;
  function(char_10, char_9);                         // se
  auto char_15 = char_6;
  print("{}{}{}",                                    // nne
        char_4, char_12, char_13);
}

// Answer: mersenne
```

**Solution 61**

```
auto function(char parameter_1, char &parameter_2) {
  print("{}",
        parameter_1);
  parameter_1 = 'p';
  char char_2{'t'};
  auto char_3 = char_2;
  parameter_2 = 'l';
  auto &char_5 = char_3;
  print("{}",
        char_5);
}
void run() {
  char char_1{'x'};
  auto char_2 = char_1;
  char char_3{'s'};
  auto char_4 = char_2;
  char_4 = 'q';
  function(char_3, char_4);                       // s
                                                  // t

  auto &char_6 = char_4;
  auto char_7 = char_2;
  char char_8{'a'};
  auto char_9 = char_3;
  char_2 = 'o';
  auto char_11 = char_3;
  auto &char_12 = char_9;
  char_1 = 's';
  auto char_14 = char_6;
  print("{}{}{}",                                 // oll
        char_2, char_4, char_6);
}

// Answer: stoll
```

**Solution 62**

```
auto function(char &parameter_1, char &parameter_2) {
  char char_1{'j'};
  print("{}",
        parameter_2);
  auto char_2 = parameter_1;
  char_1 = 'C';
  auto &char_4 = char_2;
  char_1 = 'a';
  print("{}",
        parameter_1);
}
void run() {
  char char_1{'j'};
  auto char_2 = char_1;
  char_1 = 'C';
  char char_4{'a'};
  auto &char_5 = char_4;
  char_2 = 'l';
  function(char_5, char_1);                         // C
                                                    // a
  auto &char_7 = char_5;
  char char_8{'b'};
  auto char_9 = char_2;
  char char_10{'g'};
  auto char_11 = char_7;
  char_1 = 'e';
  char char_13{'l'};
  auto char_14 = char_9;
  print("{}{}{}{}{}{}",                             // llable
        char_2, char_13, char_4, char_8, char_14, char_1);
}

// Answer: Callable
```

**Solution 63**

```
auto function(char parameter_1, char &parameter_2) {
  parameter_1 = 'l';
  char char_2{'D'};
  char_2 = 'L';
  auto &char_4 = char_2;
  parameter_1 = 'm';
  char char_6{'i'};
  print("{}",
        char_2);
}
void run() {
  char char_1{'l'};
  char_1 = 'D';
  auto char_3 = char_1;
  char char_4{'q'};
  auto &char_5 = char_1;
  auto char_6 = char_4;
  char char_7{'n'};
  auto &char_8 = char_7;
  char char_9{'w'};
  auto &char_10 = char_3;
  char_8 = 't';
  char char_12{'S'};
  char_3 = 'p';
  char char_14{'O'};
  function(char_4, char_6);                          // L
  char char_15{'w'};
  print("{}{}{}{}",                                  // ODSD
        char_14, char_1, char_12, char_5);
}

// Answer: LODSD
```

**Solution 64**

```
auto function(char &parameter_1, char parameter_2) {
  print("{}",
        parameter_1);
  parameter_1 = 's';
  char char_2{'x'};
  parameter_2 = 'p';
  auto char_4 = char_2;
  char_4 = 'a';
  print("{}",
        char_4);
}
void run() {
  char char_1{'p'};
  auto &char_2 = char_1;
  char_1 = 'p';
  auto &char_4 = char_1;
  function(char_4, char_1);                        // p
                                                   // a
  char_2 = 'a';
  auto char_6 = char_1;
  char char_7{'r'};
  auto &char_8 = char_6;
  char char_9{'d'};
  auto &char_10 = char_1;
  char_7 = 'k';
  char char_12{'h'};
  char_4 = 'g';
  char char_14{'c'};
  auto char_15 = char_12;
  char char_16{'e'};
  print("{}{}{}{}{}{}",                            // ckaged
        char_14, char_7, char_8, char_1, char_16, char_9);
}

// Answer: packaged
```

**Solution 65**

```
auto function(char &parameter_1, char parameter_2) {
  parameter_1 = 'c';
  char char_2{'.'};
  parameter_1 = 'm';
  auto &char_4 = char_2;
  char char_5{'k'};
  auto char_6 = parameter_1;
  print("{}{}",
        char_4, parameter_2);
}
void run() {
  char char_1{'c'};
  char char_2{'.'};
  auto &char_3 = char_2;
  char_3 = 'b';
  auto char_5 = char_2;
  char_2 = 'p';
  auto char_7 = char_3;
  auto &char_8 = char_3;
  auto char_9 = char_2;
  print("{}{}{}",                              // cpp
        char_1, char_9, char_7);
  char_8 = 's';
  auto char_11 = char_8;
  function(char_7, char_8);                    // .s
  char_2 = 'u';
  auto &char_13 = char_3;
  auto char_14 = char_7;
  char char_15{'j'};
  char_1 = 'x';
  char char_17{'t'};
  print("{}{}{}{}",                            // ubst
        char_3, char_5, char_11, char_17);
}

// Answer: cpp.subst
```

**Solution 66**

```
auto function(char parameter_1, char &parameter_2) {
  parameter_1 = 'W';
  parameter_1 = 's';
  print("{}",
        parameter_2);
  parameter_1 = 'x';
  char char_4{'C'};
  auto &char_5 = char_4;
  print("{}",
        char_4);
}
void run() {
  char char_1{'W'};
  char char_2{'k'};
  auto char_3 = char_1;
  auto &char_4 = char_2;
  char_3 = 'Q';
  auto char_6 = char_1;
  auto &char_7 = char_1;
  char_6 = 'c';
  char char_9{'q'};
  auto &char_10 = char_9;
  char_10 = 'P';
  char char_12{'E'};
  function(char_12, char_10);                          // P
                                                       // C
  char_2 = 'M';
  char char_14{'e'};
  auto &char_15 = char_6;
  auto char_16 = char_7;
  print("{}{}{}{}{}",                                  // MPEQW
        char_4, char_9, char_12, char_3, char_1);
}

// Answer: PCMPEQW
```

**Solution 67**

```
auto function(char &parameter_1, char &parameter_2) {
  print("{}",
        parameter_2);
  print("{}",
        parameter_1);
  parameter_1 = 'a';
  parameter_1 = 'a';
  char char_3{'r'};
  print("{}",
        char_3);
}
void run() {
  char char_1{'u'};
  auto char_2 = char_1;
  char char_3{'r'};
  char_3 = 'r';
  auto &char_5 = char_3;
  char_5 = 'v';
  auto char_7 = char_5;
  char char_8{'a'};
  char_3 = 't';
  auto &char_10 = char_2;
  char_2 = 'i';
  char char_12{'i'};
  auto char_13 = char_1;
  char char_14{'y'};
  char_13 = 'e';
  function(char_8, char_7);                          // v
                                                     // a
                                                     // r

  char char_16{'n'};
  auto char_17 = char_8;
  char char_18{'a'};
  print("{}{}{}{}",                                  // iant
        char_2, char_8, char_16, char_5);
}

// Answer: variant
```

**Solution 68**

```
auto function(char &parameter_1, char parameter_2) {
  parameter_1 = ':';
  char char_2{'y'};
  auto &char_3 = parameter_1;
  auto char_4 = parameter_2;
  char char_5{'a'};
  auto char_6 = char_3;
  print("{}{}{}{}",
        char_5, char_2, parameter_1, char_3);
}
void run() {
  char char_1{':'};
  auto &char_2 = char_1;
  char char_3{'a'};
  char_3 = 'm';
  char char_5{'a'};
  char_3 = 'f';
  char char_7{'r'};
  print("{}{}",                                      // ar
        char_5, char_7);
  char_1 = 'r';
  print("{}",                                        // r
        char_1);
  auto &char_9 = char_1;
  char_9 = 'y';
  auto &char_11 = char_7;
  char_1 = 'r';
  char char_13{'l'};
  auto &char_14 = char_2;
  char char_15{'m'};
  function(char_2, char_1);                          // ay::
  char_15 = 'i';
  char char_17{'a'};
  auto char_18 = char_13;
  char_13 = 'l';
  char char_20{'m'};
  print("{}{}{}{}",                                  // fill
        char_3, char_15, char_13, char_18);
}

// Answer: array::fill
```

**Solution 69**

```
auto function(char &parameter_1, char &parameter_2) {
  parameter_1 = 'P';
  char char_2{'S'};
  parameter_2 = 'U';
  auto char_4 = parameter_1;
  char char_5{'b'};
  auto &char_6 = parameter_1;
  print("{}{}",
        char_2, char_6);
}
void run() {
  char char_1{'P'};
  print("{}",                                   // P
        char_1);
  auto &char_2 = char_1;
  function(char_1, char_2);                     // SU
  char char_3{'U'};
  auto char_4 = char_1;
  auto &char_5 = char_4;
  char_4 = 'B';
  auto char_7 = char_2;
  char_3 = 'i';
  char char_9{'U'};
  auto char_10 = char_1;
  char char_11{'h'};
  char_10 = 'q';
  char char_13{'d'};
  auto char_14 = char_7;
  auto &char_15 = char_11;
  char char_16{'S'};
  print("{}{}{}{}",                             // BUSB
        char_5, char_9, char_16, char_4);
}

// Answer: PSUBUSB
```

**Solution 70**

```
auto function(char &parameter_1, char parameter_2) {
  parameter_2 = 'e';
  char char_2{'t'};
  parameter_2 = 'x';
  char char_4{'d'};
  parameter_1 = 'g';
  auto char_6 = parameter_2;
  print("{}",
        char_2);
}
void run() {
  char char_1{'j'};
  auto char_2 = char_1;
  auto &char_3 = char_1;
  char char_4{'o'};
  auto &char_5 = char_1;
  char char_6{'q'};
  auto &char_7 = char_3;
  function(char_7, char_5);                          // t
  char char_8{'a'};
  print("{}{}",                                      // ga
        char_3, char_8);
  char_4 = 'a';
  char char_10{'i'};
  char_3 = 'i';
  char char_12{'a'};
  auto &char_13 = char_10;
  char char_14{'e'};
  char_3 = 'm';
  auto &char_16 = char_8;
  print("{}{}{}",                                    // mma
        char_1, char_5, char_12);
}

// Answer: tgamma
```

**Solution 71**

```
auto function(char &parameter_1, char parameter_2) {
  char char_1{'i'};
  auto &char_2 = char_1;
  char_1 = 's';
  print("{}{}",
        parameter_1, parameter_2);
  char char_4{'x'};
  auto char_5 = char_1;
  print("{}{}",
        char_1, char_2);
}
void run() {
  char char_1{'i'};
  auto &char_2 = char_1;
  char char_3{'s'};
  auto &char_4 = char_2;
  print("{}{}",                                   // is
        char_2, char_3);
  char char_5{'e'};
  char_1 = 'q';
  auto &char_7 = char_4;
  char char_8{'u'};
  auto &char_9 = char_5;
  auto char_10 = char_4;
  auto &char_11 = char_9;
  char_4 = 'l';
  function(char_4, char_9);                       // le
                                                  // ss
  auto char_13 = char_1;
  char_2 = 'p';
  auto &char_15 = char_1;
  char char_16{'j'};
  char_7 = 'l';
  char char_18{'a'};
  print("{}{}{}{}{}",                             // equal
        char_11, char_10, char_8, char_18, char_15);
}

// Answer: islessequal
```

**Solution 72**

```
auto function(char &parameter_1, char parameter_2) {
  char char_1{'d'};
  auto &char_2 = parameter_1;
  auto char_3 = parameter_2;
  auto &char_4 = parameter_2;
  auto char_5 = parameter_1;
  char_1 = 'i';
  print("{}{}",
        char_3, char_1);
}
void run() {
  char char_1{'y'};
  char_1 = 's';
  char char_3{'r'};
  auto char_4 = char_3;
  print("{}",                                         // s
        char_1);
  char_3 = 'c';
  auto char_6 = char_3;
  char char_7{'o'};
  char_7 = 'i';
  char char_9{'c'};
  char_1 = 't';
  auto &char_11 = char_7;
  char_6 = 'e';
  auto char_13 = char_1;
  char char_14{'o'};
  auto &char_15 = char_7;
  function(char_4, char_9);                           // ci
  char char_16{'n'};
  auto char_17 = char_11;
  char char_18{'f'};
  auto char_19 = char_6;
  print("{}{}{}{}{}{}{}",                             // entific
        char_6, char_16, char_13, char_17, char_18, char_7,
        char_3);
}

// Answer: scientific
```

**Solution 73**

```
auto function(char &parameter_1, char parameter_2) {
  char char_1{'o'};
  auto char_2 = parameter_1;
  parameter_2 = 's';
  auto char_4 = parameter_2;
  char char_5{'t'};
  char_1 = 'c';
  print("{}{}{}",
        char_4, char_5, parameter_1);
}
void run() {
  char char_1{'o'};
  auto &char_2 = char_1;
  auto char_3 = char_1;
  char char_4{'l'};
  auto &char_5 = char_4;
  char char_6{'c'};
  auto char_7 = char_4;
  auto &char_8 = char_1;
  char char_9{'r'};
  auto char_10 = char_4;
  function(char_9, char_2);                    // str
  char char_11{'u'};
  auto char_12 = char_5;
  char char_13{'w'};
  auto &char_14 = char_2;
  print("{}{}{}{}",                            // coll
        char_6, char_2, char_7, char_5);
}

// Answer: strcoll
```

**Solution 74**

```
auto function(char parameter_1, char &parameter_2) {
  char char_1{'o'};
  char char_2{'c'};
  auto char_3 = char_1;
  char_3 = 'o';
  auto &char_5 = char_3;
  auto char_6 = parameter_1;
  print("{}{}{}",
        char_1, parameter_1, char_2);
}
void run() {
  char char_1{'o'};
  char_1 = 'c';
  print("{}",                                     // c
        char_1);
  auto &char_3 = char_1;
  char char_4{'w'};
  auto &char_5 = char_3;
  auto char_6 = char_5;
  char_4 = 'e';
  auto char_8 = char_3;
  char char_9{'t'};
  char_8 = 'e';
  auto char_11 = char_9;
  auto &char_12 = char_11;
  char char_13{'n'};
  auto char_14 = char_11;
  auto &char_15 = char_11;
  auto char_16 = char_13;
  function(char_13, char_8);                      // onc
  char_3 = 's';
  char char_18{'p'};
  print("{}{}{}{}",                               // epts
        char_4, char_18, char_14, char_3);
}

// Answer: concepts
```

**Solution 75**

```
auto function(char &parameter_1, char &parameter_2) {
  parameter_2 = 'r';
  parameter_1 = 'd';
  char char_3{'n'};
  auto char_4 = parameter_1;
  char char_5{'.'};
  auto &char_6 = char_5;
  print("{}{}{}",
        char_3, char_4, char_6);
}
void run() {
  char char_1{'r'};
  print("{}",                                        // r
        char_1);
  char_1 = 'd';
  auto &char_3 = char_1;
  char_1 = 'a';
  auto char_5 = char_3;
  print("{}",                                        // a
        char_3);
  auto char_6 = char_5;
  char char_7{'t'};
  function(char_3, char_1);                          // nd.
  char char_8{'l'};
  auto char_9 = char_8;
  auto &char_10 = char_7;
  auto char_11 = char_3;
  char char_12{'n'};
  char_10 = 'e';
  char char_14{'g'};
  char_14 = 'r';
  auto char_16 = char_7;
  char char_17{'g'};
  print("{}{}{}{}{}",                                // gener
        char_17, char_10, char_12, char_7, char_14);
  char char_18{'s'};
  auto char_19 = char_9;
  print("{}{}",                                      // al
        char_6, char_9);
}
```

```
// Answer: rand.general
```

**Solution 76**

```
auto function(char parameter_1, char &parameter_2) {
  parameter_2 = 'd';
  char char_2{'c'};
  auto char_3 = char_2;
  char_3 = 'i';
  char char_5{'x'};
  char_3 = 'n';
  print("{}{}",
        parameter_2, char_2);
}
void run() {
  char char_1{'d'};
  char_1 = 'c';
  auto &char_3 = char_1;
  auto char_4 = char_3;
  char char_5{'f'};
  function(char_5, char_1);                     // dc
  char char_6{'n'};
  auto char_7 = char_5;
  char char_8{'.'};
  char_3 = 'i';
  char char_10{'l'};
  print("{}{}{}{}",                             // l.in
        char_10, char_8, char_1, char_6);
  char_8 = 's';
  char char_12{'t'};
  auto char_13 = char_8;
  char char_14{'t'};
  char_7 = 'i';
  auto &char_16 = char_7;
  char_14 = '.';
  char char_18{'l'};
  auto char_19 = char_12;
  char char_20{'i'};
  print("{}{}{}{}{}{}{}",                       // it.list
        char_7, char_12, char_14, char_18, char_3, char_13,
        char_19);
}
```

```
// Answer: dcl.init.list
```

**Solution 77**

```
auto function(char &parameter_1, char &parameter_2) {
  char char_1{'t'};
  parameter_1 = 'i';
  char char_3{'r'};
  auto &char_4 = char_1;
  print("{}",
        char_1);
  auto &char_5 = char_3;
  print("{}",
        char_5);
}
void run() {
  char char_1{'t'};
  char_1 = 'i';
  auto &char_3 = char_1;
  char char_4{'n'};
  print("{}{}",                                    // in
        char_1, char_4);
  char_3 = 'p';
  char char_6{'u'};
  char_4 = 'y';
  function(char_6, char_4);                        // t
                                                   // r
  char_4 = 'v';
  char char_9{'o'};
  auto &char_10 = char_9;
  auto char_11 = char_1;
  char char_12{'s'};
  auto &char_13 = char_10;
  char_1 = 'l';
  auto &char_15 = char_11;
  auto char_16 = char_9;
  char_3 = 'c';
  char char_18{'e'};
  auto &char_19 = char_11;
  auto char_20 = char_1;
  char char_21{'.'};
  print("{}{}{}{}{}{}{}",                          // o.scope
```

```
        char_9, char_21, char_12, char_20, char_10, char_11,
        char_18);
}

// Answer: intro.scope
```

**Solution 78**

```
auto function(char &parameter_1, char &parameter_2) {
  parameter_1 = 'y';
  parameter_1 = 'h';
  char char_3{'u'};
  parameter_1 = 'e';
  char char_5{'j'};
  char_5 = 't';
  print("{}{}",
        char_5, parameter_1);
}
void run() {
  char char_1{'y'};
  auto &char_2 = char_1;
  auto char_3 = char_1;
  char char_4{'e'};
  auto char_5 = char_2;
  auto &char_6 = char_5;
  char_5 = 'w';
  char char_8{'.'};
  auto &char_9 = char_2;
  char_5 = 'p';
  function(char_1, char_3);                    // te
  auto &char_11 = char_6;
  char char_12{'n'};
  auto char_13 = char_9;
  auto &char_14 = char_12;
  char char_15{'t'};
  auto char_16 = char_8;
  char_4 = 'm';
  auto &char_18 = char_3;
  print("{}{}{}{}{}{}{}",                      // mp.type
        char_4, char_6, char_8, char_15, char_18, char_5,
        char_1);
}
```

```
// Answer: temp.type
```

**Solution 79**

```
auto function(char parameter_1, char &parameter_2) {
  print("{}",
        parameter_1);
  char char_1{'.'};
  auto char_2 = parameter_2;
  char_2 = 'r';
  auto char_4 = parameter_2;
  char_4 = 'g';
  print("{}",
        char_2);
}
void run() {
  char char_1{'.'};
  auto char_2 = char_1;
  char_1 = 'r';
  char char_4{'e'};
  print("{}{}",                                 // re
        char_1, char_4);
  char char_5{'g'};
  auto &char_6 = char_4;
  char_6 = 't';
  auto char_8 = char_6;
  function(char_2, char_1);                     // .
                                                // r
  auto &char_9 = char_1;
  char_1 = 'i';
  char char_11{'o'};
  auto char_12 = char_1;
  char char_13{'r'};
  auto char_14 = char_4;
  char_9 = 'e';
  char char_16{'r'};
  auto &char_17 = char_4;
  char_2 = 'm';
  auto char_19 = char_11;
  auto &char_20 = char_14;
  char char_21{'e'};
  print("{}{}{}{}{}{}",                         // egiter
```

```
        char_21, char_5, char_12, char_14, char_9, char_13);
}

// Answer: re.regiter
```

**Solution 80**

```
auto function(char &parameter_1, char &parameter_2) {
  parameter_1 = 'i';
  parameter_2 = 'n';
  char char_3{'z'};
  auto &char_4 = char_3;
  parameter_1 = 's';
  char char_6{'.'};
  print("{}{}",
        char_6, parameter_2);
}
void run() {
  char char_1{'i'};
  auto char_2 = char_1;
  char char_3{'z'};
  auto &char_4 = char_2;
  auto char_5 = char_4;
  auto &char_6 = char_1;
  char char_7{'e'};
  auto char_8 = char_1;
  char char_9{'m'};
  char_4 = 'e';
  auto &char_11 = char_8;
  char_5 = 'b';
  auto char_13 = char_4;
  char char_14{'i'};
  auto char_15 = char_5;
  char_8 = 'o';
  print("{}{}{}{}{}{}",                              // zombie
        char_3, char_11, char_9, char_15, char_1, char_2);
  char_14 = 'a';
  function(char_11, char_15);                        // .n
  auto &char_18 = char_9;
  auto char_19 = char_9;
  auto &char_20 = char_9;
  print("{}{}{}{}",                                  // ames
        char_14, char_19, char_4, char_8);
```

```
}

// Answer: zombie.names
```

**Solution 81**

```
auto function(char &parameter_1, char parameter_2) {
  char char_1{'P'};
  char char_2{'G'};
  auto char_3 = parameter_1;
  char_3 = 'A';
  char char_5{'V'};
  auto &char_6 = char_3;
  print("{}{}{}{}",
        char_5, parameter_1, char_2, char_6);
}
void run() {
  char char_1{'P'};
  auto &char_2 = char_1;
  function(char_2, char_1);                       // VPGA
  auto char_3 = char_2;
  char_3 = 'A';
  auto char_5 = char_3;
  char_2 = 'b';
  char char_7{'T'};
  auto char_8 = char_1;
  char_8 = 'o';
  auto &char_10 = char_3;
  char char_11{'m'};
  auto char_12 = char_8;
  char_11 = 'H';
  auto &char_14 = char_1;
  char_8 = 'R';
  char char_16{'n'};
  char_10 = 'w';
  char char_18{'Q'};
  auto char_19 = char_8;
  auto &char_20 = char_8;
  auto char_21 = char_18;
  char char_22{'E'};
  print("{}{}{}{}{}{}",                           // THERQQ
        char_7, char_11, char_22, char_19, char_21, char_18);
}
```

```
// Answer: VPGATHERQQ
```

**Solution 82**

```
auto function(char parameter_1, char &parameter_2) {
  parameter_1 = 'd';
  parameter_1 = 'o';
  print("{}",
        parameter_2);
  parameter_2 = 'o';
  print("{}",
        parameter_1);
  parameter_2 = 'd';
}
void run() {
  char char_1{'f'};
  char_1 = 'o';
  auto char_3 = char_1;
  auto &char_4 = char_3;
  char char_5{'c'};
  char_4 = 'a';
  auto char_7 = char_3;
  function(char_1, char_5);                        // c
                                                   // o
  auto char_8 = char_1;
  char char_9{'o'};
  auto char_10 = char_7;
  char_10 = 'i';
  auto char_12 = char_5;
  char_5 = 'w';
  auto char_14 = char_10;
  auto &char_15 = char_8;
  char_12 = '_';
  auto char_17 = char_7;
  char char_18{'i'};
  auto &char_19 = char_14;
  auto char_20 = char_3;
  char char_21{'t'};
  print("{}{}{}{}{}{}",                            // _await
        char_12, char_4, char_5, char_3, char_10, char_21);
}
```

```
// Answer: co_await
```

**Solution 83**

```
auto function(char parameter_1, char &parameter_2) {
  char char_1{'i'};
  print("{}{}",
        parameter_2, char_1);
  char char_2{'t'};
  auto char_3 = parameter_1;
  auto &char_4 = parameter_1;
  auto char_5 = parameter_1;
  print("{}{}",
        char_5, char_3);
}
void run() {
  char char_1{'i'};
  char_1 = 'h';
  char char_3{'x'};
  char_1 = 'n';
  auto &char_5 = char_3;
  auto char_6 = char_1;
  char char_7{'d'};
  char_3 = 'f';
  auto char_9 = char_1;
  char char_10{'o'};
  auto &char_11 = char_10;
  char char_12{'u'};
  auto &char_13 = char_12;
  char char_14{'q'};
  char_14 = 'f';
  auto &char_16 = char_1;
  char char_17{'u'};
  auto &char_18 = char_17;
  char char_19{'w'};
  char_3 = '.';
  auto char_21 = char_9;
  function(char_14, char_7);                          // di
                                                      // ff

  char_10 = 'l';
  auto &char_23 = char_11;
  print("{}{}{}{}{}",                                 // .null
```

```
        char_3, char_6, char_13, char_10, char_23);
}

// Answer: diff.null
```

**Solution 84**

```
auto function(char &parameter_1, char &parameter_2) {
  parameter_1 = 'h';
  parameter_1 = 'l';
  char char_3{'o'};
  char_3 = 'e';
  auto &char_5 = parameter_2;
  auto char_6 = parameter_2;
  print("{}{}",
        parameter_1, char_3);
}
void run() {
  char char_1{'w'};
  auto char_2 = char_1;
  char_1 = 'o';
  auto char_4 = char_1;
  char char_5{'f'};
  char_2 = 'o';
  char char_7{'b'};
  auto char_8 = char_2;
  char char_9{'l'};
  char_5 = '.';
  char char_11{'x'};
  auto &char_12 = char_11;
  auto char_13 = char_5;
  char char_14{'u'};
  function(char_5, char_12);                        // le
  auto char_15 = char_9;
  char char_16{'b'};
  auto char_17 = char_11;
  char_16 = 'i';
  auto char_19 = char_11;
  char char_20{'b'};
  auto char_21 = char_11;
  print("{}{}{}{}{}{}",                             // x.bool
        char_17, char_13, char_20, char_1, char_8, char_15);
}
```

```
// Answer: lex.bool
```

**Solution 85**

```
auto function(char &parameter_1, char parameter_2) {
  parameter_1 = 'e';
  char char_2{'q'};
  auto char_3 = char_2;
  auto &char_4 = char_2;
  auto char_5 = char_4;
  print("{}{}{}",
        char_4, parameter_2, parameter_1);
}
void run() {
  char char_1{'e'};
  auto &char_2 = char_1;
  char char_3{'o'};
  auto char_4 = char_2;
  char_1 = 'y';
  auto &char_6 = char_2;
  auto char_7 = char_6;
  char char_8{'p'};
  auto char_9 = char_3;
  char_7 = 's';
  auto &char_11 = char_8;
  char_1 = 'u';
  function(char_3, char_2);                        // que
  char_6 = '.';
  auto char_14 = char_9;
  char char_15{'u'};
  char_3 = 'o';
  char char_17{'y'};
  auto char_18 = char_8;
  char char_19{'c'};
  auto char_20 = char_18;
  char_8 = 'n';
  auto char_22 = char_19;
  auto &char_23 = char_1;
  print("{}{}{}{}{}{}{}",                         // ue.cons
        char_15, char_4, char_6, char_19, char_14, char_11,
        char_7);
}
```

```
// Answer: queue.cons
```

**Solution 86**

```
auto function(char parameter_1, char &parameter_2) {
  parameter_1 = 'u';
  parameter_2 = 'l';
  char char_3{'p'};
  auto &char_4 = parameter_2;
  auto char_5 = char_4;
  auto &char_6 = char_4;
  print("{}{}{}",
        parameter_1, char_3, parameter_2);
}
void run() {
  char char_1{'u'};
  char_1 = 'l';
  auto &char_3 = char_1;
  char_1 = 't';
  print("{}",                                    // t
        char_3);
  char char_5{'.'};
  function(char_3, char_1);                      // upl
  auto char_6 = char_1;
  char_1 = 'p';
  auto char_8 = char_3;
  char_6 = 'm';
  auto char_10 = char_3;
  char char_11{'a'};
  auto &char_12 = char_10;
  char_8 = 'm';
  char char_14{'f'};
  auto &char_15 = char_11;
  auto char_16 = char_15;
  char_11 = 'y';
  char char_18{'l'};
  char_14 = 'x';
  auto char_20 = char_10;
  auto &char_21 = char_20;
  auto char_22 = char_14;
  auto &char_23 = char_8;
  char_14 = 'e';
```

```
  auto char_25 = char_18;
  print("{}{}{}{}{}{}{}",                          // e.apply
        char_14, char_5, char_16, char_1, char_12, char_25,
        char_11);
}

// Answer: tuple.apply
```

**Solution 87**

```
auto function(char parameter_1, char &parameter_2) {
  char char_1{'.'};
  auto &char_2 = parameter_1;
  print("{}{}",
        parameter_2, char_2);
  char_1 = 'n';
  auto &char_4 = char_1;
  auto char_5 = char_4;
  print("{}",
        char_4);
}
void run() {
  char char_1{'.'};
  char char_2{'a'};
  auto &char_3 = char_2;
  auto char_4 = char_3;
  char char_5{'g'};
  auto char_6 = char_1;
  char char_7{'r'};
  auto &char_8 = char_5;
  auto char_9 = char_8;
  char char_10{'r'};
  function(char_2, char_10);                       // ra
                                                   // n

  char_9 = 'e';
  print("{}{}{}{}",                                // ge.r
        char_5, char_9, char_6, char_7);
  char char_12{'v'};
  auto char_13 = char_2;
  auto &char_14 = char_13;
  char_13 = 'e';
  char char_16{'i'};
  char_16 = 'e';
```

```
  char char_18{'h'};
  auto &char_19 = char_18;
  char char_20{'n'};
  auto char_21 = char_19;
  print("{}{}{}{}",                        // ange
        char_4, char_20, char_8, char_13);
}

// Answer: range.range
```

**Solution 88**

```
auto function(char &parameter_1, char &parameter_2) {
  parameter_2 = 'l';
  char char_2{'c'};
  auto char_3 = char_2;
  char char_4{'s'};
  print("{}",
        char_3);
  auto &char_5 = char_4;
  print("{}",
        parameter_2);
}
void run() {
  char char_1{'l'};
  char_1 = 'c';
  auto char_3 = char_1;
  char_1 = 's';
  auto char_5 = char_1;
  char char_6{'t'};
  auto char_7 = char_6;
  char_3 = 'k';
  char char_9{'v'};
  function(char_5, char_7);                // c
                                           // l
  auto &char_10 = char_5;
  char_1 = 'c';
  auto char_12 = char_5;
  char char_13{'j'};
  auto char_14 = char_13;
  char_6 = 'a';
  char char_16{'o'};
  auto char_17 = char_6;
```

```
  char_14 = '.';
  auto &char_19 = char_13;
  auto char_20 = char_14;
  auto &char_21 = char_10;
  char_19 = 'n';
  auto &char_23 = char_16;
  auto char_24 = char_20;
  auto &char_25 = char_7;
  print("{}{}{}{}{}{}{}{}",                    // ass.conv
        char_17, char_10, char_5, char_24, char_1, char_23,
        char_19, char_9);
}

// Answer: class.conv
```

**Solution 89**

```
void run() {
  char char_1{'r'};
  auto &char_2 = char_1;
  char_2 = 'w';
  print("{}",                                  // w
        char_2);
  char_1 = 'c';
  auto char_5 = char_2;
  char_2 = 'm';
  char char_7{'i'};
  auto char_8 = char_1;
  auto &char_9 = char_1;
  char char_10{'n'};
  auto char_11 = char_5;
  char char_12{'o'};
  char_12 = 'j';
  std::swap(char_1, char_2);
  auto &char_14 = char_1;
  print("{}{}{}",                              // cin
        char_11, char_7, char_10);
}

// Answer: wcin
```

**Solution 90**

```
void run() {
  char char_1{'S'};
  auto char_2 = char_1;
  char_2 = 'x';
  auto char_4 = char_1;
  char char_5{'s'};
  auto &char_6 = char_1;
  char char_7{'y'};
  auto &char_8 = char_4;
  char_1 = 'h';
  auto char_10 = char_5;
  char_5 = 'F';
  char char_12{'v'};
  char_1 = 'k';
  auto &char_14 = char_4;
  char char_15{'L'};
  print("{}{}{}",                                   // LFS
        char_15, char_5, char_14);
}

// Answer: LFS
```

**Solution 91**

```
void run() {
  char char_1{'l'};
  print("{}",                                       // l
        char_1);
  auto char_2 = char_1;
  auto &char_3 = char_1;
  char char_4{'r'};
  char_3 = 's';
  print("{}{}",                                     // lr
        char_2, char_4);
  auto char_6 = char_3;
  auto &char_7 = char_1;
  char char_8{'f'};
  auto &char_9 = char_4;
  char_6 = 't';
  char char_11{'i'};
  char_3 = 'n';
```

```
  auto char_13 = char_11;
  char char_14{'m'};
  auto &char_15 = char_4;
  char char_16{'s'};
  print("{}{}{}{}",                          // intf
        char_11, char_3, char_6, char_8);
}

// Answer: llrintf
```

**Solution 92**

```
void run() {
  char char_1{'p'};
  char_1 = 'c';
  auto &char_3 = char_1;
  std::swap(char_1, char_3);
  char char_4{'d'};
  auto &char_5 = char_1;
  auto char_6 = char_1;
  auto &char_7 = char_1;
  auto char_8 = char_7;
  auto &char_9 = char_3;
  char_8 = 'f';
  char char_11{'e'};
  char_9 = 'i';
  auto char_13 = char_4;
  auto &char_14 = char_3;
  std::swap(char_8, char_1);
  auto char_15 = char_1;
  char char_16{'m'};
  auto char_17 = char_7;
  print("{}{}{}{}{}",                        // fdimf
        char_7, char_13, char_8, char_16, char_3);
}

// Answer: fdimf
```

**Solution 93**

```
void run() {
  char char_1{'c'};
  char_1 = 'l';
  auto char_3 = char_1;
  auto &char_4 = char_1;
  char_4 = 'r';
  auto &char_6 = char_3;
  auto char_7 = char_1;
  char_7 = 'p';
  char char_9{'v'};
  char_9 = 'o';
  char char_11{'e'};
  std::swap(char_4, char_1);
  auto &char_12 = char_6;
  auto char_13 = char_11;
  auto &char_14 = char_9;
  std::swap(char_13, char_11);
  auto char_15 = char_7;
  print("{}{}{}",                               // rel
        char_1, char_11, char_12);
  char char_16{'k'};
  auto &char_17 = char_13;
  char_13 = 's';
  auto &char_19 = char_11;
  char char_20{'_'};
  std::swap(char_11, char_1);
  char char_21{'v'};
  print("{}{}{}{}",                             // _ops
        char_20, char_9, char_7, char_17);
}

// Answer: rel_ops
```

**Solution 94**

```
void run() {
  char char_1{'t'};
  char_1 = 'p';
  char char_3{'o'};
  char_3 = 'y';
  std::swap(char_1, char_3);
  char_1 = 'w';
  char char_6{'s'};
  print("{}{}",                                   // sw
        char_6, char_1);
  char_3 = 'o';
  char char_8{'w'};
  auto char_9 = char_8;
  char char_10{'a'};
  std::swap(char_10, char_9);
  char char_11{'b'};
  char_11 = 'd';
  auto &char_13 = char_6;
  char_9 = 'j';
  char char_15{'w'};
  std::swap(char_9, char_15);
  char_15 = 't';
  char char_17{'f'};
  auto char_18 = char_1;
  char_18 = 'a';
  char char_20{'c'};
  auto &char_21 = char_18;
  char char_22{'n'};
  auto char_23 = char_9;
  auto &char_24 = char_22;
  auto char_25 = char_10;
  print("{}{}{}{}{}",                             // scanf
        char_13, char_20, char_18, char_24, char_17);
}

// Answer: swscanf
```

**Solution 95**

```
void run() {
  char char_1{'f'};
  auto char_2 = char_1;
  char_2 = 'q';
  std::swap(char_2, char_1);
  print("{}",                                          // f
        char_2);
  char_1 = 't';
  auto &char_5 = char_1;
  std::swap(char_2, char_1);
  char char_6{'u'};
  auto char_7 = char_5;
  char char_8{'f'};
  auto &char_9 = char_6;
  char_8 = 'c';
  std::swap(char_2, char_5);
  char_9 = 'e';
  print("{}{}{}",                                      // ete
        char_6, char_5, char_9);
  std::swap(char_6, char_8);
  char_2 = 'e';
  auto char_13 = char_2;
  char_7 = 'v';
  auto &char_15 = char_5;
  char_8 = 'g';
  auto &char_17 = char_7;
  std::swap(char_9, char_7);
  auto char_18 = char_5;
  auto &char_19 = char_18;
  char_6 = 'l';
  char char_21{'s'};
  auto &char_22 = char_5;
  print("{}{}{}",                                      // ste
        char_21, char_1, char_13);
  char char_23{'p'};
  char_22 = 'k';
  char char_25{'x'};
  char_22 = 'a';
  auto char_27 = char_23;
  char char_28{'t'};
  char_15 = 'e';
```

```
  auto char_30 = char_15;
  print("{}{}{}{}{}",                                  // xcept
        char_25, char_17, char_15, char_23, char_28);
}

// Answer: fetestexcept
```

**Solution 96**

```
void run() {
  char char_1{'c'};
  auto char_2 = char_1;
  char char_3{'y'};
  auto char_4 = char_3;
  char char_5{'o'};
  char_4 = 'l';
  print("{}{}",                                        // co
        char_1, char_5);
  char_1 = 'v';
  auto &char_8 = char_2;
  char_3 = 'n';
  char char_10{'q'};
  char_4 = 'd';
  auto char_12 = char_5;
  auto &char_13 = char_4;
  auto char_14 = char_1;
  char char_15{'x'};
  char_10 = 'd';
  auto char_17 = char_4;
  char char_18{'c'};
  std::swap(char_10, char_3);
  char_12 = 'c';
  auto &char_20 = char_14;
  char_18 = 'm';
  char char_22{'p'};
  char_4 = 'r';
  char char_24{'h'};
  auto &char_25 = char_5;
  char char_26{'w'};
  char_3 = '.';
  auto &char_28 = char_25;
  char_15 = 'l';
  auto char_30 = char_22;
```

```
  print("{}{}{}{}{}{}{}",                               // nv.prom
        char_10, char_14, char_3, char_22, char_4, char_28,
        char_18);
}

// Answer: conv.prom
```

**Solution 97**

```
auto function(char &parameter_1, char &parameter_2) {
  parameter_2 = 'g';
  print("{}",
        parameter_2);
  parameter_2 = 'r';
  print("{}",
        parameter_1);
  parameter_1 = 'r';
}
void run() {
  char char_1{'g'};
  auto &char_2 = char_1;
  char char_3{'r'};
  auto char_4 = char_3;
  char_1 = 'x';
  auto &char_6 = char_3;
  char char_7{'t'};
  auto &char_8 = char_3;
  std::swap(char_8, char_2);
  char_8 = 'r';
  function(char_2, char_7);                             // g
                                                        // r
  char_1 = 'e';
  char char_11{'t'};
  char_7 = 'a';
  auto char_13 = char_1;
  char char_14{'o'};
  print("{}{}{}{}{}",                                   // eater
        char_2, char_7, char_11, char_1, char_8);
}

// Answer: greater
```

**Solution 98**

```
auto function(char parameter_1, char &parameter_2) {
  char char_1{'S'};
  auto char_2 = parameter_1;
  char char_3{'N'};
  auto &char_4 = parameter_2;
  parameter_1 = 'F';
  auto &char_6 = char_1;
  print("{}{}",
        parameter_1, char_3);
}
void run() {
  char char_1{'S'};
  char char_2{'T'};
  auto &char_3 = char_2;
  auto char_4 = char_3;
  char char_5{'F'};
  auto &char_6 = char_2;
  char_3 = 'W';
  auto char_8 = char_5;
  function(char_1, char_4);                          // FN
  auto char_9 = char_5;
  char_5 = 'f';
  auto &char_11 = char_1;
  char_8 = 'w';
  auto char_13 = char_3;
  char char_14{'t'};
  print("{}{}{}{}",                                  // STSW
        char_11, char_4, char_1, char_13);
}

// Answer: FNSTSW
```

**Solution 99**

```
auto function(char parameter_1, char &parameter_2) {
  char char_1{'s'};
  char char_2{'m'};
  auto &char_3 = char_2;
  char char_4{'e'};
  parameter_2 = 'q';
  auto char_6 = char_3;
  print("{}{}{}",
        char_6, char_4, char_3);
}
void run() {
  char char_1{'s'};
  auto char_2 = char_1;
  char char_3{'f'};
  char_2 = 'e';
  auto char_5 = char_2;
  function(char_5, char_3);                         // mem
  char_5 = 'c';
  auto &char_7 = char_1;
  char_5 = 'r';
  auto char_9 = char_2;
  auto &char_10 = char_7;
  auto char_11 = char_9;
  char_3 = 'a';
  auto char_13 = char_7;
  auto &char_14 = char_9;
  auto char_15 = char_3;
  char char_16{'.'};
  auto &char_17 = char_5;
  print("{}{}{}{}",                                 // .res
        char_16, char_5, char_11, char_7);
}

// Answer: mem.res
```

**Solution 100**

```
auto function(char &parameter_1, char parameter_2) {
  std::swap(parameter_2, parameter_1);
  parameter_1 = 'u';
  std::swap(parameter_1, parameter_2);
  char char_2{'t'};
  char_2 = 't';
  auto &char_4 = parameter_1;
  print("{}{}",
        char_2, parameter_2);
}
void run() {
  char char_1{'u'};
  auto char_2 = char_1;
  std::swap(char_2, char_1);
  char char_3{'t'};
  char_1 = 'e';
  auto &char_5 = char_3;
  char char_6{'p'};
  std::swap(char_2, char_1);
  print("{}{}{}",                                 // tup
        char_3, char_1, char_6);
  auto char_7 = char_1;
  char_1 = 'l';
  std::swap(char_1, char_7);
  char char_9{'e'};
  char_6 = 'p';
  auto &char_11 = char_2;
  char char_12{'l'};
  auto char_13 = char_6;
  char_6 = 'y';
  char char_15{'m'};
  auto &char_16 = char_7;
  char char_17{'.'};
  auto &char_18 = char_12;
  print("{}{}{}",                                 // le.
        char_18, char_11, char_17);
  function(char_7, char_2);                       // tu
  print("{}{}{}",                                 // ple
        char_13, char_16, char_9);
}
```

```
// Answer: tuple.tuple
```

**Solution 101**

```
auto function(char &parameter_1, char &parameter_2) {
  parameter_2 = 'c';
  std::swap(parameter_1, parameter_2);
  char char_2{'w'};
  auto &char_3 = parameter_1;
  parameter_2 = 'q';
  char char_5{'d'};
  print("{}{}",
        char_5, char_3);
}
void run() {
  char char_1{'c'};
  char_1 = 'a';
  auto &char_3 = char_1;
  auto char_4 = char_1;
  auto &char_5 = char_3;
  auto char_6 = char_4;
  std::swap(char_3, char_4);
  function(char_6, char_5);                      // dc
  char char_7{'e'};
  auto char_8 = char_6;
  char_4 = 't';
  char char_10{'w'};
  char_5 = 'd';
  std::swap(char_4, char_3);
  char char_12{'f'};
  auto char_13 = char_10;
  char char_14{'j'};
  auto char_15 = char_3;
  char_8 = 'k';
  char char_17{'f'};
  auto char_18 = char_12;
  char_13 = '.';
  char char_20{'l'};
  char_10 = '.';
  auto &char_22 = char_7;
  print("{}{}{}{}{}{}{}{}{}",                    // l.fct.def
        char_20, char_13, char_18, char_6, char_3, char_10,
        char_4, char_7, char_17);
```

```
}

// Answer: dcl.fct.def
```

**Solution 102**

```
auto function(char &parameter_1, char parameter_2) {
  std::swap(parameter_1, parameter_2);
  char char_1{'l'};
  std::swap(parameter_2, parameter_1);
  parameter_2 = 'j';
  auto char_3 = char_1;
  char_3 = 'o';
  print("{}",
        char_3);
}
void run() {
  char char_1{'h'};
  char_1 = 'r';
  auto char_3 = char_1;
  char_3 = 'o';
  std::swap(char_3, char_1);
  char_1 = 't';
  std::swap(char_1, char_3);
  auto char_6 = char_3;
  char_6 = 'e';
  print("{}",                                    // t
        char_3);
  auto char_8 = char_1;
  char_8 = 'b';
  auto &char_10 = char_8;
  function(char_6, char_3);                      // o
  auto &char_11 = char_3;
  char char_12{'r'};
  std::swap(char_3, char_1);
  char_1 = 'o';
  auto &char_14 = char_12;
  char char_15{'b'};
  char_10 = 'p';
  auto char_17 = char_15;
  char_10 = 'l';
  char char_19{'q'};
  char_15 = 'r';
```

```
  char char_21{'j'};
  char_3 = 'q';
  auto char_23 = char_3;
  auto &char_24 = char_14;
  char_12 = 'w';
  auto &char_26 = char_12;
  char char_27{'o'};
  auto char_28 = char_6;
  print("{}{}{}{}{}{}",                               // wlower
        char_14, char_8, char_1, char_24, char_6, char_15);
}

// Answer: towlower
```

**Solution 103**

```
auto function(char parameter_1, char &parameter_2) {
  parameter_2 = 'r';
  char char_2{'c'};
  auto char_3 = parameter_1;
  print("{}",
        char_2);
  parameter_1 = 'h';
  auto char_5 = char_3;
  print("{}",
        char_3);
}
void run() {
  char char_1{'u'};
  auto &char_2 = char_1;
  auto char_3 = char_2;
  char_2 = 's';
  auto char_5 = char_1;
  char_1 = 'r';
  auto &char_7 = char_3;
  std::swap(char_2, char_5);
  auto &char_8 = char_2;
  char char_9{'p'};
  auto &char_10 = char_5;
  char char_11{'s'};
  auto &char_12 = char_5;
  char_1 = 'k';
  char char_14{'e'};
```

```
  function(char_9, char_8);                         // c
                                                    // p
  char_8 = '.';
  char char_16{'y'};
  char_7 = 'n';
  auto char_18 = char_7;
  char char_19{'j'};
  auto char_20 = char_10;
  char char_21{'r'};
  auto &char_22 = char_7;
  auto char_23 = char_9;
  char char_24{'o'};
  print("{}{}{}{}{}{}{}",                           // p.error
        char_23, char_2, char_14, char_12, char_20, char_24,
        char_21);
}

// Answer: cpp.error
```

**Solution 104**

```
auto function(char parameter_1, char &parameter_2) {
  char char_1{'n'};
  auto &char_2 = parameter_1;
  parameter_1 = 'c';
  auto &char_4 = char_2;
  parameter_1 = 'u';
  print("{}{}",
        char_4, char_1);
}
void run() {
  char char_1{'n'};
  char char_2{'d'};
  char_1 = 'c';
  auto char_4 = char_1;
  auto &char_5 = char_4;
  auto char_6 = char_4;
  auto &char_7 = char_4;
  char char_8{'m'};
  function(char_2, char_1);                         // un
  auto &char_9 = char_8;
  char char_10{'e'};
  auto &char_11 = char_9;
```

```
  auto char_12 = char_2;
  char char_13{'t'};
  char_2 = 'x';
  auto &char_15 = char_10;
  char char_16{'e'};
  auto char_17 = char_16;
  auto &char_18 = char_16;
  char char_19{'p'};
  std::swap(char_9, char_4);
  auto &char_20 = char_2;
  auto char_21 = char_1;
  auto &char_22 = char_12;
  print("{}{}{}{}{}{}{}{}",                        // expected
        char_16, char_2, char_19, char_15, char_6, char_13,
        char_17, char_12);
}

// Answer: unexpected
```

**Solution 105**

```
void run() {
  char char_1{'d'};
  auto &char_2 = char_1;
  auto char_3 = char_1;
  char_1 = 'P';
  auto char_5 = char_2;
  char_3 = 'M';
  char char_7{'j'};
  auto char_8 = char_2;
  char char_9{'O'};
  char_2 = std::exchange(char_5, char{'C'});
  char char_11{'F'};
  auto char_12 = char_5;
  char char_13{'s'};
  print("{}{}{}{}{}{}",                            // FCOMPP
        char_11, char_5, char_9, char_3, char_1, char_2);
}

// Answer: FCOMPP
```

**Solution 106**

```
void run() {
  char char_1{'y'};
  auto char_2 = char_1;
  char char_3{'D'};
  char_2 = 'F';
  auto char_5 = char_3;
  char char_6{'r'};
  char_6 = 'A';
  auto &char_8 = char_5;
  auto char_9 = char_3;
  auto &char_10 = char_6;
  char char_11{'b'};
  auto &char_12 = char_11;
  auto char_13 = char_3;
  print("{}{}{}{}",                                  // FADD
        char_2, char_6, char_13, char_3);
}

// Answer: FADD
```

**Solution 107**

```
void run() {
  char char_1{'l'};
  char char_2{'c'};
  char_1 = 'r';
  print("{}",                                        // c
        char_2);
  auto &char_4 = char_2;
  char char_5{'h'};
  auto char_6 = char_4;
  char_2 = std::exchange(char_1, char{'e'});
  char char_8{'p'};
  char_4 = std::exchange(char_2, char{'c'});
  auto char_10 = char_2;
  char char_11{'o'};
  char_4 = 'e';
  char char_13{'a'};
  auto char_14 = char_13;
  char char_15{'s'};
  auto &char_16 = char_13;
```

```
  char_14 = 'm';
  char char_18{'v'};
  print("{}{}{}{}{}{}",                              // ompare
        char_11, char_14, char_8, char_16, char_10, char_1);
}

// Answer: compare
```

**Solution 108**

```
void run() {
  char char_1{'m'};
  char char_2{'l'};
  char_1 = 'o';
  char char_4{'a'};
  char_2 = std::exchange(char_1, char{'a'});
  auto &char_6 = char_2;
  char_4 = 'P';
  char char_8{'O'};
  auto &char_9 = char_6;
  char_2 = 'y';
  auto &char_11 = char_4;
  char char_12{'A'};
  char_1 = std::exchange(char_6, char{'q'});
  auto char_14 = char_11;
  char_6 = std::exchange(char_2, char{'d'});
  auto char_16 = char_2;
  char_16 = 'v';
  auto char_18 = char_6;
  auto &char_19 = char_11;
  char char_20{'e'};
  auto &char_21 = char_14;
  print("{}{}{}{}",                                  // POPA
        char_19, char_8, char_4, char_12);
}

// Answer: POPA
```

**Solution 109**

```
void run() {
  char char_1{'i'};
  auto char_2 = char_1;
  char char_3{'e'};
  auto char_4 = char_2;
  char_1 = std::exchange(char_2, char{'.'});
  char char_6{'l'};
  auto char_7 = char_6;
  char char_8{'s'};
  char_6 = 'x';
  char_3 = std::exchange(char_2, char{'n'});
  auto char_11 = char_7;
  char_6 = 'i';
  char char_13{'s'};
  char_7 = 't';
  auto &char_15 = char_11;
  char_11 = 'v';
  char char_17{'e'};
  char_13 = 's';
  print("{}{}{}{}{}",                              // intse
        char_4, char_2, char_7, char_13, char_17);
  char_15 = 'u';
  char char_20{'q'};
  char_20 = std::exchange(char_7, char{'w'});
  char char_22{'q'};
  char_17 = std::exchange(char_1, char{'q'});
  char_11 = 'e';
  auto &char_25 = char_2;
  char char_26{'o'};
  print("{}{}{}{}",                                // q.in
        char_22, char_3, char_6, char_25);
  auto char_27 = char_1;
  print("{}{}{}{}",                                // tseq
        char_20, char_8, char_15, char_27);
}

// Answer: intseq.intseq
```

**Solution 110**

```
void run() {
  char char_1{'c'};
  auto &char_2 = char_1;
  char_1 = std::exchange(char_2, char{'i'});
  char char_4{'h'};
  print("{}",                                           // c
        char_1);
  char char_5{'r'};
  auto char_6 = char_4;
  char_6 = std::exchange(char_4, char{'o'});
  char char_8{'l'};
  auto char_9 = char_5;
  print("{}{}{}",                                       // hro
        char_6, char_9, char_4);
  char_1 = ':';
  auto char_11 = char_8;
  char char_12{'n'};
  char_11 = 'y';
  auto &char_14 = char_5;
  char char_15{'b'};
  char_4 = 'i';
  auto &char_17 = char_1;
  char_14 = 'o';
  char char_19{'a'};
  print("{}{}{}{}",                                     // no::
        char_12, char_14, char_2, char_17);
  char_14 = 'j';
  auto char_21 = char_4;
  char char_22{'s'};
  auto &char_23 = char_12;
  char char_24{'m'};
  print("{}{}{}",                                       // abs
        char_19, char_15, char_22);
}

// Answer: chrono::abs
```

**Solution 111**

```
void run() {
  char char_1{'h'};
  char_1 = 'j';
  char char_3{'m'};
  char_1 = 'e';
  char char_5{'t'};
  auto char_6 = char_5;
  char char_7{'h'};
  auto &char_8 = char_1;
  char char_9{'i'};
  char_3 = 's';
  char char_11{'a'};
  auto char_12 = char_11;
  char_1 = 'k';
  auto char_14 = char_6;
  auto &char_15 = char_3;
  char char_16{'c'};
  char_1 = 'p';
  auto char_18 = char_1;
  char_14 = 'g';
  char_14 = std::exchange(char_1, char{'j'});
  auto &char_21 = char_6;
  char char_22{'n'};
  char_14 = std::exchange(char_18, char{'s'});
  print("{}{}{}{}{}{}",                                  // static
        char_18, char_5, char_12, char_21, char_9, char_16);
  char char_24{'x'};
  auto char_25 = char_8;
  char_24 = '_';
  char_8 = std::exchange(char_6, char{'f'});
  char char_28{'c'};
  char_22 = 't';
  char char_30{'c'};
  print("{}{}{}{}{}",                                    // _cast
        char_24, char_30, char_11, char_3, char_22);
}

// Answer: static_cast
```

**Solution 112**

```
void run() {
  char char_1{'b'};
  auto &char_2 = char_1;
  char_2 = 'e';
  char char_4{'s'};
  auto &char_5 = char_4;
  print("{}",                                          // s
        char_5);
  char char_6{'h'};
  auto &char_7 = char_5;
  auto char_8 = char_2;
  auto &char_9 = char_4;
  char_4 = 'g';
  char char_11{'n'};
  auto &char_12 = char_8;
  char char_13{'q'};
  char_6 = 'd';
  char char_15{'g'};
  auto &char_16 = char_12;
  char char_17{'p'};
  auto char_18 = char_1;
  char_16 = 'y';
  char char_20{'j'};
  auto &char_21 = char_7;
  char char_22{'w'};
  char_12 = std::exchange(char_9, char{'w'});
  char_4 = 't';
  auto &char_25 = char_4;
  char_20 = 'x';
  char char_27{'u'};
  print("{}{}{}{}{}{}",                                // tudent
        char_25, char_27, char_6, char_18, char_11, char_7);
}

// Answer: student
```

**Solution 113**

```
auto function(char &parameter_1, char parameter_2) {
  char char_1{'i'};
  char_1 = 'r';
  char char_3{'s'};
  parameter_1 = 'b';
  char char_5{'s'};
  parameter_1 = 'o';
  print("{}{}",
        char_3, parameter_2);
}
void run() {
  char char_1{'i'};
  auto &char_2 = char_1;
  auto char_3 = char_1;
  char char_4{'y'};
  char_2 = std::exchange(char_3, char{'s'});
  char char_6{'o'};
  print("{}{}",                                  // io
        char_1, char_6);
  char_1 = 'g';
  char char_8{'s'};
  char_4 = 'a';
  auto &char_10 = char_8;
  char char_11{'b'};
  std::swap(char_6, char_4);
  char char_12{'a'};
  auto &char_13 = char_1;
  char char_14{'_'};
  char_4 = std::exchange(char_3, char{'j'});
  char char_16{'f'};
  char_10 = std::exchange(char_4, char{'n'});
  function(char_2, char_14);                     // s_
  auto &char_18 = char_8;
  char char_19{'e'};
  auto &char_20 = char_11;
  print("{}{}{}{}",                              // base
        char_11, char_12, char_10, char_19);
}

// Answer: ios_base
```

**Solution 114**

```
auto function(char &parameter_1, char &parameter_2) {
  parameter_1 = 'k';
  parameter_2 = 'c';
  char char_3{'o'};
  parameter_1 = 'j';
  print("{}{}",
        parameter_2, char_3);
  char char_5{'n'};
  print("{}",
        char_5);
}
void run() {
  char char_1{'d'};
  auto &char_2 = char_1;
  char char_3{'o'};
  auto char_4 = char_1;
  char_3 = 'n';
  auto &char_6 = char_3;
  char char_7{'p'};
  char_4 = 'k';
  auto char_9 = char_1;
  char char_10{'k'};
  auto char_11 = char_4;
  char_10 = std::exchange(char_9, char{'q'});
  char_2 = 'n';
  auto &char_14 = char_9;
  char_2 = 'j';
  auto char_16 = char_3;
  auto &char_17 = char_14;
  std::swap(char_16, char_6);
  function(char_17, char_1);                           // co
                                                       // n
  char_17 = std::exchange(char_2, char{'v'});
  auto char_19 = char_17;
  char char_20{'a'};
  char_6 = 'r';
  char char_22{'.'};
  char_9 = 'e';
  auto &char_24 = char_2;
  print("{}{}{}{}{}{}",                                // v.rank
        char_1, char_22, char_3, char_20, char_16, char_4);
```

```
}

// Answer: conv.rank
```

**Solution 115**

```
auto function(char parameter_1, char &parameter_2) {
  parameter_1 = 'e';
  parameter_2 = std::exchange(parameter_1, char{'y'});
  char char_3{'m'};
  char_3 = 'n';
  auto &char_5 = char_3;
  auto char_6 = char_3;
  print("{}{}",
        parameter_2, char_6);
}
void run() {
  char char_1{'e'};
  auto char_2 = char_1;
  char char_3{'q'};
  auto char_4 = char_2;
  char_3 = 'l';
  char char_6{'c'};
  char_4 = 'a';
  char char_8{'g'};
  print("{}{}{}",                               // leg
        char_3, char_1, char_8);
  auto char_9 = char_2;
  char char_10{'l'};
  function(char_4, char_3);                     // en
  auto char_11 = char_9;
  char char_12{'j'};
  char_1 = 'c';
  std::swap(char_6, char_9);
  auto char_14 = char_6;
  char_9 = 'y';
  char char_16{'x'};
  auto &char_17 = char_11;
  char_1 = 'd';
  char_4 = std::exchange(char_3, char{'h'});
  char char_20{'d'};
  char_1 = 'u';
  char_11 = std::exchange(char_8, char{'f'});
```

```
  auto &char_23 = char_8;
  char char_24{'r'};
  print("{}{}{}{}",                              // drel
        char_20, char_24, char_6, char_10);
}

// Answer: legendrel
```

**Solution 116**

```
auto function(char &parameter_1, char &parameter_2) {
  char char_1{'e'};
  auto &char_2 = parameter_2;
  auto char_3 = char_2;
  char char_4{'d'};
  char_3 = 'u';
  parameter_1 = std::exchange(char_1, char{'r'});
  print("{}{}",
        parameter_2, char_3);
}
void run() {
  char char_1{'e'};
  auto char_2 = char_1;
  char char_3{'q'};
  char_1 = 'd';
  char char_5{'u'};
  char_5 = 'v';
  char char_7{'c'};
  auto char_8 = char_5;
  auto &char_9 = char_2;
  auto char_10 = char_9;
  std::swap(char_5, char_9);
  function(char_10, char_3);                     // qu
  char_8 = std::exchange(char_10, char{'n'});
  auto char_12 = char_9;
  char_2 = std::exchange(char_3, char{'e'});
  auto char_14 = char_3;
  char_12 = 'a';
  char_2 = std::exchange(char_14, char{'j'});
  auto &char_17 = char_7;
  char char_18{'l'};
  auto char_19 = char_5;
  char_3 = std::exchange(char_19, char{'k'});
```

```
  char_19 = 'u';
  char_8 = std::exchange(char_7, char{'.'});
  function(char_12, char_3);                          // eu
  char_19 = std::exchange(char_12, char{'s'});
  auto &char_24 = char_10;
  char_12 = 'u';
  auto &char_26 = char_14;
  auto char_27 = char_9;
  char_8 = 'x';
  char_26 = std::exchange(char_24, char{'f'});
  auto &char_30 = char_3;
  print("{}{}{}{}{}{}",                               // e.defn
        char_30, char_7, char_1, char_2, char_24, char_26);
}

// Answer: queue.defn
```

**Solution 117**

```
auto function(char &parameter_1, char parameter_2) {
  char char_1{'m'};
  char char_2{'o'};
  auto &char_3 = char_1;
  std::swap(parameter_2, char_1);
  char char_4{'g'};
  print("{}{}",
        parameter_2, char_1);
}
void run() {
  char char_1{'m'};
  auto &char_2 = char_1;
  char char_3{'h'};
  std::swap(char_3, char_2);
  auto char_4 = char_1;
  std::swap(char_2, char_4);
  char char_5{'e'};
  function(char_3, char_5);                           // me
  char_4 = 'f';
  char_3 = std::exchange(char_2, char{'i'});
  char_1 = '_';
  char char_9{'u'};
  auto &char_10 = char_4;
  char char_11{'n'};
```

```
  char_3 = 'r';
  char char_13{'1'};
  auto &char_14 = char_1;
  function(char_13, char_1);                          // m_
  char_1 = 'n';
  char_4 = std::exchange(char_9, char{'_'});
  auto char_17 = char_9;
  char char_18{'p'};
  auto &char_19 = char_18;
  char char_20{'d'};
  std::swap(char_2, char_1);
  auto &char_21 = char_4;
  char_11 = 'f';
  auto &char_23 = char_18;
  auto char_24 = char_9;
  char_9 = 'n';
  char_19 = std::exchange(char_2, char{'t'});
  char char_27{'f'};
  print("{}{}{}{}{}{}",                               // fun1_t
        char_27, char_10, char_9, char_13, char_24, char_14);
}

// Answer: mem_fun1_t
```

**Solution 118**

```
auto function(char &parameter_1, char parameter_2) {
  parameter_1 = std::exchange(parameter_2, char{'u'});
  parameter_2 = 't';
  parameter_1 = std::exchange(parameter_2, char{'n'});
  char char_4{'p'};
  auto &char_5 = parameter_1;
  char char_6{'w'};
  print("{}{}",
        char_4, char_5);
}
void run() {
  char char_1{'o'};
  char char_2{'t'};
  char_1 = 'o';
  auto char_4 = char_1;
  auto &char_5 = char_4;
  std::swap(char_1, char_2);
```

```
  char char_6{'x'};
  char_4 = 'p';
  auto char_8 = char_5;
  std::swap(char_5, char_4);
  auto char_9 = char_6;
  auto &char_10 = char_6;
  char char_11{'c'};
  std::swap(char_1, char_10);
  auto char_12 = char_5;
  auto &char_13 = char_8;
  char_11 = 'd';
  auto char_15 = char_6;
  auto &char_16 = char_8;
  char_5 = std::exchange(char_8, char{'i'});
  char_5 = 'f';
  function(char_16, char_1);                          // pt
  char_12 = 'e';
  char char_20{'i'};
  auto char_21 = char_10;
  char_6 = std::exchange(char_5, char{'_'});
  auto &char_23 = char_4;
  char_2 = 't';
  std::swap(char_13, char_6);
  char_9 = std::exchange(char_20, char{'d'});
  auto &char_26 = char_20;
  char_1 = 'r';
  char char_28{'i'};
  print("{}{}{}{}{}{}{}",                             // rdiff_t
        char_1, char_11, char_9, char_13, char_16, char_23,
        char_6);
}

// Answer: ptrdiff_t
```

**Solution 119**

```
auto function(char parameter_1, char &parameter_2) {
  print("{}",
        parameter_2);
  parameter_1 = std::exchange(parameter_2, char{'u'});
  parameter_2 = 't';
  parameter_2 = std::exchange(parameter_1, char{'e'});
  print("{}",
        parameter_1);
  parameter_2 = 't';
}
void run() {
  char char_1{'n'};
  char_1 = 't';
  auto char_3 = char_1;
  auto &char_4 = char_1;
  char_4 = std::exchange(char_3, char{'e'});
  char char_6{'r'};
  std::swap(char_6, char_3);
  auto char_7 = char_4;
  char char_8{'e'};
  char_8 = 'k';
  auto &char_10 = char_1;
  char char_11{'b'};
  auto &char_12 = char_10;
  std::swap(char_3, char_11);
  auto char_13 = char_8;
  char_13 = 'i';
  auto char_15 = char_6;
  std::swap(char_7, char_13);
  function(char_12, char_11);                       // r
                                                    // e
  auto char_16 = char_10;
  auto &char_17 = char_7;
  char_13 = '.';
  char char_19{'o'};
  char_12 = 'd';
  char_12 = std::exchange(char_17, char{'o'});
  auto &char_22 = char_16;
  char_3 = 'o';
  char char_24{'r'};
  auto char_25 = char_13;
```

```
  auto &char_26 = char_17;
  auto char_27 = char_1;
  print("{}{}{}{}{}{}{}{}",                          // .tokiter
        char_13, char_22, char_26, char_8, char_27, char_11,
        char_6, char_24);
}

// Answer: re.tokiter
```

**Solution 120**

```
auto function(char &parameter_1, char parameter_2) {
  parameter_2 = 'm';
  std::swap(parameter_2, parameter_1);
  char char_2{'q'};
  char_2 = 'm';
  auto &char_4 = char_2;
  auto char_5 = parameter_2;
  print("{}",
        parameter_2);
}
void run() {
  char char_1{'m'};
  auto char_2 = char_1;
  auto &char_3 = char_1;
  char char_4{'f'};
  auto char_5 = char_1;
  char char_6{'f'};
  auto char_7 = char_6;
  char char_8{'g'};
  function(char_6, char_1);                          // f
  std::swap(char_2, char_1);
  auto &char_9 = char_8;
  char_7 = 'k';
  char char_11{'u'};
  function(char_11, char_5);                         // u
  char char_12{'l'};
  auto char_13 = char_3;
  char_2 = 'p';
  auto &char_15 = char_1;
  char char_16{'.'};
  std::swap(char_3, char_9);
  char_11 = 'n';
```

```
  char_12 = std::exchange(char_4, char{'p'});
  auto char_19 = char_13;
  char_3 = 'e';
  auto char_21 = char_4;
  char_6 = 'y';
  char char_23{'n'};
  auto &char_24 = char_5;
  char char_25{'l'};
  char_5 = std::exchange(char_3, char{'c'});
  auto char_27 = char_5;
  print("{}{}{}{}{}{}{}{}",                          // nc.memfn
        char_11, char_1, char_16, char_9, char_24, char_13,
        char_12, char_23);
}

// Answer: func.memfn
```

**Solution 121**

```
auto function(char &parameter_1, char parameter_2) {
  parameter_2 = 's';
  char char_2{'i'};
  print("{}",
        parameter_2);
  char char_3{'c'};
  char_3 = std::exchange(char_2, char{'e'});
  auto &char_5 = char_3;
  print("{}",
        char_2);
}
void run() {
  char char_1{'s'};
  char_1 = 'w';
  char char_3{'x'};
  char_3 = 'e';
  auto &char_5 = char_3;
  char char_6{'u'};
  auto char_7 = char_3;
  char char_8{'y'};
  std::swap(char_6, char_5);
  auto &char_9 = char_3;
  char_6 = 'd';
  char char_11{'r'};
```

```
  char_3 = 'q';
  auto &char_13 = char_7;
  std::swap(char_9, char_1);
  char char_14{'s'};
  char_5 = 'e';
  char char_16{'i'};
  char_11 = 'n';
  std::swap(char_11, char_9);
  auto char_18 = char_16;
  char_7 = 'o';
  char char_20{'f'};
  auto &char_21 = char_14;
  char char_22{'_'};
  auto &char_23 = char_20;
  char_8 = 'b';
  char char_25{'a'};
  auto char_26 = char_22;
  function(char_5, char_21);                          // s
                                                      // e
  auto &char_27 = char_16;
  char_18 = std::exchange(char_16, char{'e'});
  auto &char_29 = char_6;
  print("{}{}{}{}{}{}",                               // ed_seq
        char_27, char_6, char_26, char_14, char_16, char_1);
}

// Answer: seed_seq
```

**Solution 122**

```
auto function(char &parameter_1, char &parameter_2) {
  char char_1{'l'};
  auto &char_2 = char_1;
  char_1 = 'x';
  auto &char_4 = parameter_2;
  char_1 = 'o';
  print("{}",
        parameter_1);
}
void run() {
  char char_1{'a'};
  auto char_2 = char_1;
  char_2 = 'r';
```

```
    auto char_4 = char_2;
    char_4 = 'i';
    char_4 = std::exchange(char_2, char{'a'});
    char char_7{'n'};
    auto char_8 = char_2;
    char_1 = '.';
    auto &char_10 = char_4;
    char char_11{'r'};
    auto char_12 = char_2;
    char char_13{'e'};
    function(char_11, char_2);                          // r
    char char_14{'m'};
    char_2 = std::exchange(char_1, char{'s'});
    auto char_16 = char_7;
    function(char_8, char_1);                           // a
    std::swap(char_10, char_16);
    char char_17{'d'};
    auto char_18 = char_1;
    print("{}{}{}{}{}",                                 // nd.en
          char_7, char_17, char_2, char_13, char_10);
    char_2 = 'h';
    auto &char_20 = char_2;
    auto char_21 = char_14;
    char char_22{'.'};
    auto char_23 = char_21;
    char_8 = 'r';
    char char_25{'e'};
    auto char_26 = char_10;
    char char_27{'g'};
    char_10 = 'r';
    auto &char_29 = char_8;
    print("{}{}{}{}{}{}",                               // g.mers
          char_27, char_22, char_14, char_25, char_11, char_1);
}

// Answer: rand.eng.mers
```

**Solution 123**

```
auto function(char parameter_1, char &parameter_2) {
  parameter_2 = 'e';
  parameter_2 = 'p';
  char char_3{'x'};
  auto char_4 = parameter_1;
  print("{}",
        char_3);
  auto &char_5 = char_4;
  print("{}",
        parameter_2);
}
void run() {
  char char_1{'e'};
  print("{}",                                            // e
        char_1);
  auto &char_2 = char_1;
  char char_3{'x'};
  auto char_4 = char_3;
  auto &char_5 = char_2;
  char char_6{'c'};
  auto char_7 = char_4;
  char char_8{'d'};
  std::swap(char_6, char_1);
  auto &char_9 = char_5;
  char char_10{'c'};
  auto &char_11 = char_1;
  std::swap(char_11, char_6);
  char char_12{'m'};
  auto &char_13 = char_12;
  char char_14{'m'};
  char_3 = '.';
  auto char_16 = char_14;
  auto &char_17 = char_7;
  char_11 = std::exchange(char_10, char{'a'});
  auto &char_19 = char_8;
  char_6 = 'o';
  function(char_12, char_17);                            // x
                                                         // p

  auto &char_21 = char_9;
  char char_22{'p'};
  char_17 = std::exchange(char_16, char{'j'});
```

```
  auto &char_24 = char_22;
  char_12 = 'r';
  char char_26{'y'};
  auto &char_27 = char_13;
  print("{}{}{}{}{}{}{}",                             // r.comma
        char_13, char_3, char_11, char_6, char_17, char_14,
        char_10);
}

// Answer: expr.comma
```

**Solution 124**

```
auto function(char &parameter_1, char &parameter_2) {
  std::swap(parameter_2, parameter_1);
  parameter_2 = 'm';
  char char_2{'k'};
  std::swap(parameter_2, char_2);
  auto &char_3 = parameter_2;
  char char_4{'t'};
  print("{}",
        char_2);
}
void run() {
  char char_1{'m'};
  auto &char_2 = char_1;
  char_1 = 'g';
  char char_4{'y'};
  function(char_2, char_1);                          // m
  char_4 = std::exchange(char_1, char{'e'});
  char_4 = 'e';
  char char_7{'q'};
  auto &char_8 = char_1;
  print("{}",                                        // e
        char_2);
  char_4 = 'v';
  auto &char_10 = char_7;
  char char_11{'n'};
  auto char_12 = char_11;
  char_10 = '.';
  char char_14{'y'};
  char_2 = std::exchange(char_11, char{'w'});
  auto char_16 = char_1;
```

```
  char_12 = 'r';
  auto char_18 = char_7;
  char_10 = 'a';
  auto char_20 = char_10;
  std::swap(char_12, char_11);
  auto &char_21 = char_16;
  auto char_22 = char_8;
  char_1 = 't';
  char char_24{'m'};
  auto &char_25 = char_14;
  auto char_26 = char_11;
  char char_27{'u'};
  char_16 = 'l';
  auto char_29 = char_26;
  char_16 = 'n';
  char char_31{'x'};
  char_31 = 't';
  char char_33{'k'};
  auto char_34 = char_27;
  print("{}{}{}{}{}{}{}{}",                          // ta.unary
        char_8, char_20, char_18, char_34, char_21, char_10,
        char_29, char_14);
}

// Answer: meta.unary
```

**Solution 125**

```
auto function(char &parameter_1, char parameter_2) {
  parameter_2 = std::exchange(parameter_1, char{'l'});
  char char_2{'y'};
  parameter_1 = 'W';
  std::swap(char_2, parameter_1);
  char char_4{'A'};
  print("{}{}",
        char_2, char_4);
}
void run() {
  char char_1{'e'};
  char char_2{'k'};
  char_2 = 'W';
  std::swap(char_2, char_1);
  char_2 = 'A';
```

```
  char_2 = std::exchange(char_1, char{'A'});
  print("{}",                                            // W
        char_2);
  char char_6{'t'};
  auto &char_7 = char_2;
  char_7 = 'h';
  auto &char_9 = char_1;
  auto char_10 = char_1;
  char_7 = 'F';
  auto char_12 = char_6;
  char char_13{'/'};
  auto char_14 = char_13;
  std::swap(char_10, char_1);
  char_13 = 'I';
  auto char_16 = char_1;
  char_6 = std::exchange(char_1, char{'T'});
  auto &char_18 = char_7;
  print("{}{}{}{}{}",                                    // AIT/F
        char_16, char_13, char_1, char_14, char_7);
  char char_19{'I'};
  auto &char_20 = char_10;
  char char_21{'a'};
  char_10 = 'i';
  auto char_23 = char_6;
  auto &char_24 = char_12;
  char_1 = '-';
  char char_26{'T'};
  function(char_14, char_24);                            // WA
  char char_27{'i'};
  auto &char_28 = char_12;
  char char_29{'W'};
  auto char_30 = char_12;
  char char_31{'r'};
  auto &char_32 = char_1;
  print("{}{}{}{}{}{}{}",                                // IT-Wait
        char_19, char_26, char_32, char_29, char_21, char_27,
        char_12);
}

// Answer: WAIT/FWAIT-Wait
```

**Solution 126**

```
auto function(char &parameter_1, char &parameter_2) {
  parameter_2 = 'f';
  char char_2{'p'};
  parameter_1 = 'e';
  auto char_4 = char_2;
  std::swap(parameter_2, char_4);
  auto char_5 = parameter_2;
  print("{}",
        parameter_1);
}
void run() {
  char char_1{'n'};
  auto char_2 = char_1;
  char char_3{'e'};
  auto &char_4 = char_3;
  char_4 = std::exchange(char_3, char{'d'});
  auto char_6 = char_1;
  std::swap(char_6, char_2);
  char_6 = 'n';
  auto char_8 = char_3;
  char char_9{'t'};
  auto &char_10 = char_4;
  auto char_11 = char_6;
  char char_12{'q'};
  auto &char_13 = char_10;
  auto char_14 = char_11;
  char_2 = 'v';
  auto &char_16 = char_8;
  auto char_17 = char_16;
  std::swap(char_9, char_10);
  char char_18{'c'};
  char_6 = 'e';
  auto char_20 = char_8;
  char char_21{'x'};
  std::swap(char_2, char_3);
  char_10 = 'v';
  char char_23{'r'};
  char_13 = '.';
  auto char_25 = char_16;
  char char_26{'v'};
  auto &char_27 = char_11;
```

```
  function(char_27, char_9);                        // e
  auto &char_28 = char_27;
  char_16 = 'p';
  auto &char_30 = char_11;
  char_12 = 'q';
  auto &char_32 = char_23;
  print("{}{}{}{}{}{}{}{}{}",                       // xcept.pre
        char_21, char_18, char_28, char_9, char_2, char_10,
        char_16, char_32, char_30);
}

// Answer: except.pre
```

**Solution 127**

```
auto function(char parameter_1, char &parameter_2) {
  parameter_1 = 's';
  parameter_1 = std::exchange(parameter_2, char{'h'});
  std::swap(parameter_1, parameter_2);
  parameter_1 = 'u';
  char char_4{'t'};
  auto &char_5 = parameter_1;
  print("{}",
        char_5);
}
void run() {
  char char_1{'y'};
  auto char_2 = char_1;
  std::swap(char_1, char_2);
  char char_3{'u'};
  char_1 = 'd';
  char char_5{'i'};
  char_3 = 'c';
  auto &char_7 = char_3;
  std::swap(char_2, char_1);
  char_1 = std::exchange(char_2, char{'f'});
  auto &char_9 = char_2;
  char_3 = 'd';
  auto &char_11 = char_7;
  char_1 = 'a';
  auto char_13 = char_3;
  std::swap(char_13, char_9);
  char_2 = 'e';
```

```
  auto char_15 = char_1;
  char_3 = 'm';
  auto char_17 = char_2;
  char_11 = 'l';
  auto char_19 = char_5;
  char char_20{'v'};
  std::swap(char_7, char_19);
  char_2 = '.';
  auto &char_22 = char_7;
  char_3 = 'h';
  auto char_24 = char_5;
  char char_25{'n'};
  auto &char_26 = char_17;
  char_20 = 'b';
  auto &char_28 = char_15;
  char char_29{'y'};
  char_1 = 'd';
  auto &char_31 = char_11;
  std::swap(char_11, char_28);
  auto char_32 = char_15;
  std::swap(char_22, char_28);
  auto char_33 = char_31;
  function(char_19, char_5);                        // u
  auto &char_34 = char_33;
  char_3 = 'd';
  auto &char_36 = char_24;
  char_19 = 'a';
  char_19 = std::exchange(char_26, char{'d'});
  char char_39{'x'};
  print("{}{}{}{}{}{}{}{}",                         // axid.def
        char_28, char_39, char_36, char_17, char_9, char_7,
        char_19, char_13);
}

// Answer: uaxid.def
```

**Solution 128**

```
auto function(char &parameter_1, char parameter_2) {
  char char_1{'o'};
  std::swap(parameter_2, char_1);
  char_1 = 'l';
  parameter_1 = std::exchange(char_1, char{'.'});
  std::swap(parameter_1, char_1);
  char char_4{'a'};
  print("{}{}",
        char_1, parameter_2);
}
void run() {
  char char_1{'o'};
  auto &char_2 = char_1;
  char_2 = '.';
  char char_4{'a'};
  auto char_5 = char_4;
  function(char_2, char_4);                       // lo
  auto &char_6 = char_2;
  char_6 = std::exchange(char_1, char{'w'});
  auto char_8 = char_6;
  char char_9{'j'};
  char_5 = 'a';
  std::swap(char_1, char_9);
  auto &char_11 = char_5;
  auto char_12 = char_8;
  char_5 = 'l';
  auto &char_14 = char_11;
  char_8 = 'e';
  auto &char_16 = char_9;
  char_6 = std::exchange(char_4, char{'e'});
  auto char_18 = char_8;
  char char_19{'f'};
  auto &char_20 = char_2;
  auto char_21 = char_16;
  char_21 = 't';
  char_21 = std::exchange(char_2, char{'b'});
  char_19 = 'c';
  auto &char_25 = char_16;
  auto char_26 = char_25;
  char char_27{'y'};
  auto &char_28 = char_26;
```

```
  char char_29{'l'};
  auto &char_30 = char_4;
  std::swap(char_5, char_21);
  char_20 = 'r';
  auto &char_32 = char_21;
  char char_33{'n'};
  std::swap(char_2, char_20);
  auto &char_34 = char_4;
  char_25 = 'c';
  char_26 = std::exchange(char_20, char{'l'});
  char_9 = 'g';
  char char_38{'e'};
  print("{}{}{}{}{}{}{}{}{}{}{}{}",                 // cale.general
        char_19, char_5, char_32, char_18, char_12, char_16,
        char_30, char_33, char_4, char_28, char_14, char_29);
}

// Answer: locale.general
```

www.ingramcontent.com/pod-product-compliance
Lightning Source LLC
LaVergne TN
LVHW060821170826
845678LV00010B/1859

* 9 7 9 8 8 1 7 2 6 8 7 3 7 *